It's Not Always
Black And White

CAUGHT
BETWEEN
TWO
WORLDS

DR. JOHN REED

outskirtspress
DENVER, COLORADO

Dr. John Reed
Website: doctorjohnreed.com
Email: doctorjohnreed@gmail.com
FaceBook: Dr. John Reed
Twitter: @docjohnreed

Cover Photo © 2013 JupiterImages Corporation. All rights reserved - used with permission.
Author Photo by Danielle M. Wooten, Photographer of Berryfotogenicphotography.com.

Outskirts Press, Inc.
http://www.outskirtspress.com

ISBN: 978-1-4787-1669-3

Outskirts Press and the "OP" logo are trademarks belonging to Outskirts Press, Inc.

PRINTED IN THE UNITED STATES OF AMERICA

To

Tiana

John

and

Nico

Words cannot ever explain the love I have for you!

Always,

Your Father

Acknowledgement

It has been a long and eventful journey turning this book into reality. *It's Not Always Black and White* most certainly would still be a dream without the help and encouragement from a small but devoted group of supporters.

Foremost, I want to thank my wife, Lisa, for her undying love, support, and patience throughout this particular journey. Dealing with me during this time was certainly not easy; yet, she shouldered the various duties of critic, cook, chauffeur, children's teacher, sounding board, to name only a few of many, with genuine excitement and sincerity.

I also would like to applaud my three youngest children, Tiana, John, and Nico. As such an undertaking of writing a book naturally occupied much of my time, their patience and understanding is greatly appreciated. It is especially with them in mind, that I wrote this book.

A much heartfelt thank-you to my 'Brother' and best friend Konstantin Konstantinidis (Coco). His courage and honesty gave me the strength to stand up for myself and break the shackles that held me down. It must not have been easy to watch how I was being treated, which makes his unwavering love and support for me even more special.

A warm thank-you to my father in-law Maarten Couwenberg whose advise and guidance has been with me from the start. Whether reviewing parts of my manuscript or helping me scanning photos for the book, he always took the time to assist me whenever needed.

Finally, great thanks go to my editor Lee Ann for tightening my manuscript and shaping it into the book it is today. Her editing work in conjunction with her valuable opinions and suggestions are greatly appreciated.

Table of Contents

Introduction

"CAN I TAKE your order, Fräulein?" the waiter asked curtly. His chilly demeanor was in stark contrast to the beautiful spring day we were enjoying. The sky was blue, the sun was shining brightly, and the air was warm; not the norm for this time of the year in Germany. My mother, who was a white woman, had separated from my African-American father, and had decided to take me on a trip. We stopped at a restaurant for lunch. *What a great day this is,* I thought, my six-year-old mind never imagining that it could (and would) turn so ugly.

Looking over a menu, my mother decided on the potato soup, which excited me, because it was my favorite. She ordered a bowl for each of us. Without responding, the waiter scribbled on a piece of paper and marched off. He was gone for what seemed like a very long time, and after a while, I began noticing that other tables were being served, even though they arrived well after we had. That seemed strange to me, but I was excited regardless, as potato soup was one of my favorites. My mother was becoming fidgety, clearly ill at ease.

Finally the waiter came back and without a word, put a single bowl of soup in front of my mother. "Where is the other potato soup?" my mother asked. "There is only one soup for you. We will only serve you here," he replied coldly. He was sending a clear message, and my mother's face quickly reddened. I had seen that same look when she was mad at me, so I knew that something had to be wrong. I held my breath, afraid, and not daring to move a muscle. All I wanted was to have a taste of that delicious soup that was in front of us, but it was not to be. My mother angrily snatched me by the hand and whisked me away, while my stomach growled in protest. I was disappointed to say the least, but I was also filled with a sense of shame and anger that I couldn't fully grasp, and didn't completely understand. In fact, it would not be until many years later that I would begin to comprehend that the restaurant incident had nothing to do with my mother, and everything to do with me.

Certain situations I remembered as a child, now look different to me as an adult. As a child, I believed that most insults were just that; insults, and nothing more. I now understand that many of these insults were racially motivated. Understandably, I was unable to comprehend this reality then, as I would be able to later, due to life experience. This is how I am certain I did not fully interpret racist confrontations as such. However, as an adolescent, life begins to take on another dimension. It is a time for establishing one's identity. I tried to answer the question, *Who am I?* in hopes that I could establish a coherent sense of self. For biracial individuals, the question is more complicated, because of the two different heritages, resulting in the fact that the potential for identity confusion is bigger.

How I define a situation is based on my personal history, expectations, and feelings. This in turn determines how I behave. Clearly, I lacked personal history to understand the incident described above, but I am sure that my feelings and expectations were greatly influenced by this incident. People see things differently at particular times, and as they develop cognitively, physically, and psychosocially, they will see the same phenomenon differently throughout their life span.

The purpose of this book is to share my story (a story experienced by innumerable biracial individuals) and use myself as an example in the hope of giving other people permission to be courageous enough to be open and honest about their struggles. You are not alone.

As you will discover later in the book, biracial individuals faced many challenges in the past. Even though the consensus is that they do not face these challenges anymore, it is not true. Sadly, challenges such as racism, discrimination, and lack of social acceptance, to name a few, are still very much a part of the lives of many biracial individuals today; a fact that is supported in detail in the following chapters.

The following is a story of how I journeyed from a lost child, to becoming a man who found his legitimate place in this world. It is to be hoped that my story will provide an insight into the world of people with multiple racial heritages, and impart a better understanding of people's challenges with low self-esteem, self-worth, and lack of social acceptance.

This is a very personal story insofar as I will bare my soul. I would not have it any other way, since I want you to be able to better understand my journey. Yes, I will be vulnerable, but what a great way to show true strength. I am not afraid to share my deepest sorrows with you if, in the end, it will serve its purpose: to be of help to you, to find your strength and live a better life. From as early as I can remember, my life has been about finding acceptance, and the fact that I had to fight for my own mother's acceptance complicated my life even more.

Those who knew me during my childhood might be surprised to read that I was this insecure, low self-esteem kind of person, because all I showed back then was the opposite: a confident and secure person. That is how I survived.

This book is divided into four parts: in part one, I will present a brief background about my family. Then in part two, I will reveal details about my life. Part three will present some information about society's past and current racial issues. Finally in part four, I hope to inspire you to make the changes necessary for you to live the life you want to live.

To avoid confusion for the reader, I will use the terms biracial and multiracial interchangeably.

My story begins in a southern German town, Schwäbisch Gmünd, in the early sixties. Interestingly, my journey on this planet began with a twist. Not only did three different doctors tell my mother she was unable to conceive, but when I was born, I almost died due to the umbilical cord being wrapped around my neck and suffocating me. Well, if those weren't signs that my life would be full of obstacles.

However, before we dive into my story, allow me to give a little background information about my family.

PART 1

Family Background

MY MATERNAL GRANDPARENTS, Andreas and Pauline Perlak (Oma and Opa), used to live in what was then called Sudeten Deutschland, a part of the former Czech Republic. From there, they moved by way of Austria to Germany, to the town of Schwäbisch Gmünd. They arrived in 1946, and lived there with 7 of their 13 children in a wood cabin in the forest. In 1958, Opa built a house at Schindelackerweg 61.

My memories of Opa are kind. I remember sitting on his lap playing games, and how he would cuddle me. He would send me to the store to get Chantre (a type of brandy) for him. Knowing how much he loved his Chantre made me feel so honored that he trusted me to get it for him. Being that I was only 6 years old, going to the store to get liquor for my grandfather might seem unusual, but it was not an uncommon thing in those days. Plus, the store owner knew me and my grandfather, so it was no problem. Opa was a chain smoker, which eventually led to his death in 1970 due to lung cancer.

Oma died 16 years later, in 1986. My relationship with her as a child was okay. As I got older though, especially during my teenage years, the relationship between us grew very strong. I fondly remember our lunches, where she would tell me stories from the past that helped me understand her and our family better. I told Oma that my mother used to tell me that Opa did not care for me because of my skin color. Oma acted surprised. "No, he adored you," she assured me. I was so relieved to hear that Opa cared for me, because it confirmed the deep feelings of love I felt from him.

Grandfather and Big Mama

The story about my paternal grandparents carries a little surprise; however, it is a surprise that surfaces in the history of many Black families in America. The Reed family can be traced back to Jerry Reed and Jane, whose family name is unknown. Jerry was of Scottish and Irish heritage, and Jane was of Choctaw Indian and White heritage. Choctaw Indians are recognized as one of the United States' original native tribes. Jane was classified as Black, and they were not allowed to marry; so they lived together under "common law" (a system of law that is derived from judges, rather than constitutions).

Jane and Jerry had two children, one of whom was my grandfather, John David Reed. John had eight children with his first wife, and five with his second one, who happened to be my grandmother, Caroline Hickman, affectionately called "Big Mama." Together they had five children, including my father, John David Reed II.

Looking at both sides of my family, clearly the (skin) color White is prevalent. What is even more amazing is that the (skin) color Black was not introduced into the family until my grandfather, John David Reed, Sr., married and had offspring with his second wife, Caroline Hickman. Undoubtedly, if Black families were to dig a little into their family history, they would most likely discover that somewhere along the line there was white DNA introduced into the gene pool.

My Parents

As history tells us, after World War II the allies occupied Germany. My father, John Reed Jr., who was from Mississippi, found himself stationed in Schwäbisch Gmünd in the late fifties. Sometime after his arrival, he met my mother, Wilhelmine Perlak, and they started a relationship. The relationship between my parents turned bad just before he was deployed back to the U.S. It just so happened that right before he left, my mother became pregnant with me. Upon telling my father, he did not believe her, thinking that she was just trying to keep him committed to her, remembering he was told she was unable to have children. So my father went back to the States.

After I was born, my mother sent a picture of me to my father. Any doubts he may have had that I was his son were erased when his mother saw the picture and proclaimed that I, indeed, was his son. Having proof now in his hands, my father went back to Germany, and eventually married my mother.

PART 2

Life Before Self-Discovery

I CAN REMEMBER being very quiet, shy and some would say well-mannered when I was a young child. The reason for this behavior was because I did not want to rock the boat. I did not want to draw any more attention to myself than I already did. In doing so, I was trying to please everyone, especially my mother. As I got older, I gained confidence through sports. Soccer and track and field were my favorite sports, and I especially excelled in soccer.

So from the beginning, the big challenge for me was to see where I could fit in. Though I spoke the same language, I was treated differently, no matter what I did. My skin color was brown, a fact I could not hide. Though my friends treated me well, others, who did not know me, treated me with racial attitudes.

The earliest memory of my childhood goes back to one particular incident when I was around three years old. I remember being in the hallway of the house that my grandfather had built, surrounded by my mother, grandmother, aunt, great-grandmother, and my older cousin Eddie. I had gotten into trouble. Crying, I went to Eddie, and he took me into his arms and consoled me. We formed a strong bond early on, which was going to stay this way throughout our teenage years. Unfortunately, one particular incident years later changed our relationship.

I spent the first eleven months of my life in a convent, where I was taken care of by nuns. It seems that rejection came early for me.

Why was I taken care of by others rather than my own mother? It is a question that I have asked myself countless times; and it is a question that has never been answered. Though I'd like to believe that being single and having to work, my mother was (somehow) forced to have others take care of me, based on my childhood experience with her, I have arrived at a different conclusion. More about that later. I cannot attest to my father's parenting skills, but I want to believe that he loved me. He told me a little story that went like this: when he finally got to visit me in the convent, he was told that I would not take to him, since I was surrounded only by women and was scared of men. However, when he picked me up, I looked at him and did not cry. This surprised everybody. I'd like to believe that it was a natural bond I had with my father.

It is a similar story that I encountered when my first son, Tahi, was born. During the pregnancy, I would often say, *"Hello this is your Papa speaking."* When he was born, he cried like babies do. The nurse handed him to me, and I spoke the same words I had been speaking to him all those months. Upon hearing my voice, Tahi turned his little head, looked at me, and stopped crying. It was a very profound moment for me. I can only imagine that this is how my father felt when he first saw me. I mention this at this point to paint a better picture for the story that follows.

First Time Living in America

As stated previously, my mother and father decided to get married shortly after he returned to Germany. When I was a baby, we lived in a couple of German towns before relocating to the United States, moving to Fort Bragg, North Carolina. I don't remember much of this time spent in America, but I do remember meeting my grandmother, Big Mama, and a sister of mine who I did not even know existed. Also, I remember meeting family in Ohio. My father was gone a lot. It was during this time in America that I learned to fear my father. I learned to fear him through my mother, who made him out to be a very strict, callous, and no-nonsense man. She also tried to convince me that it was he who beat me. I say convince, because I do not remember my father ever spanking me. This tactic of putting fear into me was something my mother used throughout my childhood, until the day I knew better.

I do remember receiving beatings from my mother from an early age. She used leather belts, shoes, sticks, her hand; whatever was convenient. Many times she spanked me with a wooden cooking spoon. One day, after finally having enough of being spanked with that spoon, I snatched it from her and broke it across my knee. I thought that was the end of it; but the next time, my mother just used a much thicker wooden spoon, one that I was not able to break. Well, I tried.

My Parents Separate

After the short stay in America, we went back to Germany. For reasons unknown to me, my parents weren't able to manage to stay together. When I was around four years old, they separated again; this time for good. The pain of being abandoned by my father was excruciating. I felt rejected. It is a pain I haven't forgotten to this day, and has affected every decision I've ever made in life since, whether consciously or unconsciously. I did not see my father until more than thirteen years later. "Why did you not take me with you?" I asked when I finally saw him. "Oh Johnny, I wanted to, but your mother would not let me." Her decision to keep me proved to have far-reaching implications that would come to rear their ugly heads in very painful manners for years to come. It would be an underlying theme that would affect me greatly during my entire upbringing.

The fact that my mother refused to let me live with my father would seem natural. I mean, most mothers would decide to keep their child. Though I would like to believe that my mother decided to keep me because she loved and wanted the best for me, I know this is not true. The only reason she decided to keep me was to hurt my father. Knowing the love my father had for me was her way of getting even with him. That is how much she hated him. Something I would continually be reminded of throughout my life.

By making this decision, she did not realize that not only would she hurt him, but she would also hurt herself, and especially me. The fact that she had a child with a black man was something for which she never forgave herself. It did not help that in Germany, such a union met with disapproval. She therefore was not allowed to live a normal life. The ramifications of that decision were to affect me deeply. Her hatred, disgust, frustration, and disappointment about the relationship with my father was something she directed toward me. Furthermore, finding acceptance was compounded by society's refusal to see me as one of their own.

Living in Germany without my father left me without a role model. From what I can remember, I was very close to him. He would take me with him wherever he went. I did not understand what the repercussions would be of my father leaving; he was the only person I could identify with. Whereas I probably would have confidently explored the world more openly with his support, I retreated into a shell, allowing my mother to take over my life. It would take many years, incredible effort, but most of all brutal honesty, to crack that shell.

Trying to Find a Home

After my mother and father separated, we moved around a lot; never having a steady home. Right after my father left, we lived with some friends of ours who had a biracial daughter. They treated me very well, surely having to do with the fact that their daughter was biracial.

We then moved in with my mother's sister, Tante Gina, and stayed there for a year. Living with Tante Gina, her husband and their two children was interesting, to put it mildly. On one hand, I enjoyed living there, because I didn't feel so lonely. On the other hand, while my cousins were treated like royalty, I was treated as the proverbial fifth wheel. There is one incident that stands out in my mind to illustrate this.

Frau Münch

My cousins and I usually played together outside, because I was not really allowed to play in the house with them. It was mid-afternoon, and I was by myself, sitting in front of the house. Sitting on the ground, I was rocking back and forth, a habit I had developed whenever I felt sad and lonely. It was a way of comforting myself, and is a habit that has stayed with me until this day. I was hungry, and my stomach was growling because I had not eaten since breakfast. Our neighbor, Frau Münch, noticed that I was sitting outside. "Johnny, are you hungry?" she asked. "Yes," I answered, somewhat hesitantly. "Would you like something to eat?" she continued. "Yes," I said, as softly as I could, so Tante Gina would not hear me. "Come on in please. I will fix you some lunch." Inside her house, I sat at the kitchen table while she made an egg and toast for me. What a welcome sight, to see and smell the warm food! While I was eating, Tante Gina came outside looking for me, I guess because she couldn't see me sitting in front of the house anymore. Probably wondering where I was, she called my name, and Frau Münch responded, "Johnny is here with me, eating lunch. I will send him over when he is done."

The food tasted so good, and my tummy was satisfied. I wish I could have enjoyed lunch a little more, but I hurried, because I had a feeling that Tante Gina was not pleased that Frau Münch fed me. I was to find out just how right I was. "Thank you, Frau Münch," I said sadly. I did not want to go back to Tante Gina's, but I knew I had no other choice. Sensing that I was sad, Frau Münch hugged me and with a soft voice said, "Johnny, you can come back again soon. I love you."

The look on Tante Gina's face when she opened the door scared me. She was very angry, and told me to go straight to bed. *What?* I thought. *It's only 3 o'clock in the afternoon. All this because Frau Münch gave me food?* When my mother finally came home around five o'clock, I was still in bed. She did not say much. There was no defense, no questions, no actions on my behalf. If I felt bad before, I surely felt worse now.

The year we spent at Tante Gina's house was a year full of tension. Besides being neglected by her and my extended family, my mother neglected and beat me for no apparent reason more times than I care to remember. Driving in the car with Tante Gina, my mother, and my cousins one day, my cousins were loud, and would not stop, despite being told to by their mother to be quiet. Riding along, looking out of the window and minding my own business, I suddenly felt a sting on my face. My mother had slapped me, hard. I was shocked! I had done nothing! The anger I saw in her face shut me down. I did not dare to complain, for fear things would get worse. Years later, when we were adults, my cousin told me, "I remember that ride in the car, when your mother slapped you even though you did not do anything. Johnny, we all knew and talked about how badly your mother treated you. Sorry." Wow, I had no idea. Yet, no one came to my rescue.

I was in my own lonely world. Feeling this way was normal to me. Interestingly, I developed a peculiar habit. When I would go out and play, I would often pick up a rock or a stick. That in itself was not a problem. What was strange was that once I picked up a rock or a stick, I couldn't put it down anymore. A sad feeling came over me, believing that the rock or stick was lonely too. *Don't worry. I'll take care of you. I won't abandon you,* I thought. Feeling guilty, I would take them home with me. I could not let go because I thought if I did, they would be as lonely as I was, and I couldn't stand the thought of that. You should have seen the collection of things I amassed over time.

Moving In with Oma

In April of 1970, Opa died. Oma, now living alone in that big house, invited us to move in with her. My mother found a job on the Army base, and would usually get home about five o'clock. That was okay, because my grandmother was there. However, that changed whenever my grandmother went to visit relatives, which meant that she would be gone for weeks at a time. Again, that in itself would not have been a big deal, but you see, I used to get home from school around twelve thirty, since school was over at noon every day. So here I am, the proverbial latchkey kid, coming home around twelve thirty to an empty house, having to feed and look after myself. Talk about growing up quickly.

How alone I was while growing up became really clear one particular day. Playing in the woods with my friends, we used to break these tree branches against their trunks, and the pieces would fly through the air. That was fun, until on one occasion; a piece hit me right on my temple. Oh, how that hurt! I just took off running for home, crying all the way. I can still remember the snot running down my nose, and the tears streaming down my cheeks.

I made it! I cried in my mind. I turned the key in the lock and walked inside, ready to be hugged, ready to be loved. *Mama, where are you? I got hit in the head and it hurts so bad!* The words screamed through my mind, but nothing happened. When I walked in the house, nobody was there. I was greeted by emptiness and darkness. I felt so alone. I just balled up in a corner somewhere, crying, waiting for Mama to come home.

What remains deeply embedded in my heart and memory is the coldness and loneliness I felt the moment I walked into that empty house. To this day, I can feel the sadness I felt so many years ago. That little boy who got hurt that day is still inside of me. To be honest, I don't want to forget what I felt that day. It has allowed me to be more sensitive to the feelings of others, and I will do my part so others won't have to feel this emptiness.

Biracial Peers

In the town where I grew up, there were several other biracial kids. Unfortunately for them, they lived in a part of town known as the ghetto. They had two major strikes against them: one, they lived in the ghetto and two, they were Black. Wherever they went, their status and reputation would precede them, and the fact that they could not hide their skin color, did not help. That, of course, was a major disadvantage. Fortunately for me, I did not live in that part of town. In addition, being a well-known soccer player and attending a good school allowed me to enjoy a status and respect my biracial peers could only dream of. Still, I was not spared from racial attacks and disrespect. Imagine what my peers went through.

Thinking back though, I am convinced that without my athletic abilities, I would have been treated like my biracial peers. It seems that only when a person of color is of use to White society, will they receive better treatment. Surely, that was true in my case. Status or social class is said to influence the degree of social acceptance for people of color. It did in my case.

If affluent, which I was not, or being able to contribute a skill that is above-average to society, which I did, being a top soccer player, status increases. In contrast, people of color who were poor and did not contribute a skill above-average, fared rather poorly. Even though I am certain that being the only biracial student in high school elevated my status, I would like to believe that my personality added to my likability.

My Stepfather

After many years of my mother and I having been alone, she started dating again. The man she started seeing was a G.I. He was a white man from Texas, who would eventually become my stepfather. Unfortunately for him, he was mistreated by my mother, something he did not deserve. Yelling at him or talking down to him was a constant occurrence, and not once did I see him being allowed to make his own decision. As a teenaged boy trying to establish myself as a man, watching how my mother treated him the way she did was very frustrating for me. But most disturbing to me was that he would not stand up to her; defend himself the way he should have. I did not like what

I saw, and told my mother. Her only response was, "No man will ever treat me the way your father did." She was so wrong for treating him like this, and I am happy to say that he eventually got smart enough to leave her.

In the summer of 1974, my mother went to Texas to marry him. I spent the summer at Tante Gina's house. Though I had never had any racial issues with my stepfather while he was dating my mother, Tante Gina stirred the pot. During a conversation one day, she hinted, "Your stepfather is from Texas, and might have a problem with you being Black." "Oh," was all I could muster. Not quite sure how to take this, I kept it to myself, and never told my mother about it.

Somehow, months later in a conversation about Tante Gina, the subject came up about race, and I told my mother, "Tante Gina told me that Dad might have a problem with me being Black." What I did not know is that Tante Gina voiced the same concern to Oma, who confirmed what I said. My mother confronted Tante Gina and, as a result, they had a big argument. They did not speak to each other for years. My stepfather, to his credit, treated me like I was his own son. There weren't any racial issues with him, contrary to what Tante Gina said. However, the following story illustrates how race seemed to always be an issue with my mother.

While on a vacation in Austria, we stayed in a small village. One afternoon, deciding to go for a little walk through the village, we came upon a group of young kids. Seeing me, they approached me gingerly, staring at me, hardly believing their eyes that they were seeing a person of color. It went so far that one of the kids approached and poked me to see if I was real. It infuriated my mother. I, on the other hand, did not mind at all, because I knew the kids meant no harm. I tried to reason with my mother, but she would have none of it. Rather than ensuring me that all was okay, she took offense to the action, and unknowingly made me feel much worse.

Years later, when we had moved to Fort Bragg, this time with my stepfather, a similar incident happened. This one, however, was much more positive for me. It wasn't for my mother. We were walking outside a grocery store when a couple of black girls passed us. As the girls were passing, they started screaming like they were at a Michael Jackson concert, apparently liking my looks. I was not used to this, and was slightly embarrassed. I would be lying though if I said that I did not like what happened. My mother and I both turned in the direction of the girls. Whereas I enjoyed the situation, she reacted in disbelief. She looked at the girls, and then at me, and said disapprovingly, "Because of you?" I just shrugged and responded, "I guess?" Her comment and facial expression told me it was not a compliment. It was an insult.

The reason I took it as an insult was because for as long as I can remember, my mother spoke unkindly about black people, and especially about my father. She was constantly telling me, "Your father and black people are no good." How do you deal with such negative comments on a continuous basis? Subconsciously, I internalized those statements. Is it a wonder then with this history, I automatically interpreted the above comment negatively. It would take many years to unravel (most) of the damage my mother caused.

Due to my mother's issue with my skin color, I believed that I was unattractive, which did not help my self-esteem. To appear more attractive, I tried to look more White. Some of you may have seen the movie Malcolm X. In the movie, Malcolm X (played by Denzel Washington) did everything he could, even enduring great pain, to straighten his hair, to appear more like a white person. All because he was ashamed of who he was. This is a classic example of self-hatred.

Now my dear readers, you may think that this is only a movie. Well, allow me to enlighten you. My hair is very curly. I didn't know I had curls until my teenage years, because from as far back as I can remember, my mother would always comb my hair straight. I kept that habit throughout childhood and adolescence. I straightened my hair to appear acceptable, that is, to appear more White. I was too ashamed to show my curls, despite receiving compliments when people did get a chance to see them. For instance, coming out of the pool one day, a girl commented, "Johnny, you have such pretty curls. Why do you comb you hair straight instead of letting it be curly?" Though I appreciated the compliment, I had no response, and continued to straighten my hair. So you see, self-hatred is real, and so is the constant bombardment of reminders that Whites and their way of life '*Is the way.*'

Summertime

An interesting observation during the summertime was how many of the German people reacted when they saw me. "What a beautiful color you have. I wish I could be that brown." Miraculously, I was *admired* for my skin color! Yet, I knew it was only a show, and would be forgotten the rest of the year, when those people who wished they could be brown in summertime were able to hide their bodies and pale skin. How hypocritical, desiring to be brown and fighting that desire at the same time.

Billions of dollars are spent every year for tanning. To me, that accentuates the desire of white people to have color. The following question, then, deserves a closer look: a*re white people unhappy with their skin color?* Surely you have heard people say, "You don't look so good today. You look pale; get some color." What about the obsession with chocolate, not to mention that America's favorite drinks, for example, coffee, whisky, and coke, are dark? Is this a method of getting some color?

Additionally, it is a fact that Black is the color of power. One only has to look at what judges, business men, or grooms are wearing. What about cigars and cigarettes? Do powerful business men smoke big, dark cigars, or small, white cigarettes? Finally, is it not true that tall, dark, and handsome men are the preferred mate for countless white women?

Considering the before-mentioned, is that why people of color are discriminated against? After all, this is a *White Man's World*, and any threat to eliminate Whiteness is desperately fought against. Let's contemplate another question for a moment: could it be that racism and prejudice, which are strongest against Black people, are in reality the frustration of not having something that one so desires? I believe this is called reaction formation. Just look at the examples above. What do you think?

Finally, here is an intriguing reason why racism and prejudice is strongest against Black individuals, in particular against black men: black men have the greatest genetic potential to influence the appearance of all other races, especially the White race. So to assure white genetic survival, black men are attacked, discredited, and destroyed. Now, who really has the power?

Let's not get off track here; but know that I will cover why racism is still a problem today later in the book.

First Real Girlfriend

Like a teenager with normal urges, I yearned to have a girlfriend. Though I did not have many girlfriends, I was able to experience a couple of relationships. I met a girl in the next town over whom I dated for almost a year. According to her and her friends, her mother was prejudiced, and did not approve of our relationship. It seemed I was walking on eggshells whenever I was visiting my girlfriend. Oddly enough, the times I *did* run into her mother, which were usually on the city bus, never resulted in a confrontation. I can't even tell you for sure whether those statements about her mother were true. There is the possibility that she may not have felt this way; nonetheless, the impression was given to me that she was a racist, and this did not help my self-worth.

My Heart Gets Broken

Then there was the girl in my class who was very fond of me. We would see each other quite often, though she lived across town. Before her, I had dated a girl from my class, which led to much hand-holding. All the experiences with the girls in my class were like puppy loves. It was not until I was sixteen, that I had a girlfriend who I really fell for. She was the stereotypical German girl; blond hair, blue eyes, and white skin. It was the relationship with this girl that was to change my world view and at the same time, shatter my heart.

One day my mother said, "I had a talk with your girlfriend's mother. We spoke about you." "Good," I responded, believing what was to come next would be a good thing. I had no inkling of an idea how wrong I would be. "Gabi's mother thinks you are a fine young man." My heart jumped for joy. Then it shattered. "Nonetheless, she won't allow any serious relationship between the two of you, because you are Black." To explain the pain I felt when I heard this is not possible. It was at that very moment I understood, *No matter what I did, and no matter how I spoke, I would never be seen as an equal among the German people.*

So there I was, of White and Black heritage, being reinforced that neither my white nor my black heritage, is accepted. What it really meant is that *I* am not accepted. My self-worth and self-esteem were virtually nonexistent. There is the belief among minorities that being White in this society automatically guarantees better treatment and unearned benefits and privileges. That having white skin allows you the freedom to choose the neighborhood or school you want to live in or attend, since you won't be discriminated against. Considering my experience, it is true.

Being not only biracial but also bicultural, I can tell you this phenomenon is true in Germany also. Going shopping one day, I entered a store and was being followed by a sales person from the second I entered. I, of course, was aware of that, so I allowed myself to have a little fun with this situation. Purposely, I walked from one end of the store to the other, repeatedly. The sales person continuously followed. Finally, the sales person stopped following me. Now, of course you may say that this behavior wasn't necessarily racially motivated. I beg to differ for two reasons: one, there were other (white) patrons in the store whom the sales person totally ignored, being too busy following me. Two, not once did the sales person ask whether I needed help, especially since I seemed to be lost in the store.

High School

I had a blast in high school. I guess since I was the only black kid in school, I enjoyed a certain status. High school is where my athletic abilities really paid dividends. It was also the six years of my life where bonds were formed that are still in place today.

In the fifth grade, I entered the Adalbert-Stifter-Realschule (ASR). It was the beginning of the six-year segment that would have a huge effect on me. It was a time during which I formed more of an understanding of my place in society, which was to be altered many years down the road; and it was also during this time that both great memories and devastating ones were made.

I established myself at the top of the class with another boy, Joe. Being one of the oldest, it seemed natural to be a leader. In addition, my athletic forays would cement my status in high school, and would do the same for me in my town and region. More about that later. Being popular in school was addicting. Finally, I found a place where I was accepted and felt I belonged. It was also a place where I felt safe. My classmates knew how I felt about the times back in high school, and I also shared this with one of our teachers, Frau Schiele, at a class reunion in 2009. She, in turn, surprised me with her own story.

At that class reunion in 2009, we had the pleasure of having Frau Schiele among us. She had been the vice principal at ASR, and was known to be a strict teacher. She was the one who really was in charge at the school, and we all knew this. In addition, she was our English teacher. In retrospect, we now understand that as strict as she was, she taught us a lot. We had not seen her in many years; thus, the pleasure of seeing her again at the class reunion was great and mutual.

Since I had been known as the class clown, she seemed very touched and proud that I had earned my doctorate. Upon discussing the topic of my dissertation, *The Lived Experience of Racism and Discrimination Among Biracial Adults*, she was surprised that the issues discussed were real. Frau Schiele was under the impression that I did not meet with racism and prejudice while I was living in Germany.

"I remember the day you came to ASR. I knew you were biracial, but believed you would not have any problems. Still, as a precaution, I surrounded you with teachers who would protect you from students, in case it was needed." With a big smile on her face she continued, "As I had hoped for, a wonderful thing happened: your peers accepted you as one of them. Protection from your peers was never needed. That made me feel really good, Johnny," she said, with tears in her eyes.

Hearing Frau Schiele speak those words was wonderful. Looking into her eyes lovingly, I said, "Thank you." Then I told her that while I was in school, I certainly felt loved and protected. It was outside of my familiar surroundings that I met with racism. Sharing a few examples, I could see the pain in her eyes, and with a heavy voice she said, "Johnny, I want to learn more about this subject. Will you help me?" "Of course!" I nearly shouted. "It would be an honor, Frau Schiele." Even years removed from being our high school teacher, she was again teaching us one of life's great lessons: one is never too old to learn new things! So for starters, I provided her with a copy of my dissertation. We continued exchanging emails until she died. *You, Frau Schiele, served as a wonderful role model. We will always be indebted to you. Thank you.*

There is a reason why I provided the above story for you readers. I wanted to demonstrate that even in today's time, there are many people who are ignorant of the fact that racism and prejudice are still issues in society. Now when I say ignorant, I don't mean this in a disrespectful way. It is simply stated this way to underscore how important it is for people to understand that racism and prejudice are prevalent and alive today. We must all do whatever we can to eliminate such behavior, because whether we believe it or not, every person is affected by racism and prejudice one way or another. Even white people. Just ask any white person who has met with the anger and frustration of a person of color due to her or his frustration with racism and discrimination.

To demonstrate my ignorance about Black history, allow me to share the following story. At the end of my senior year in high school, I had to take an oral history exam. I remember standing in front of three teachers. Among many questions I was asked, there was one that stood out, and it was an answer that, unknowingly to me then, must have shocked the teachers. One of the teachers asked me, "What was the reason for the Civil War?" I shrugged my shoulders and said, "I have no idea." Imagine their surprise when they heard the answer. Here I was, a Black individual who had absolutely no clue about the history of his ancestry. I certainly realize now how foolish the situation must have seemed. Believe me, I would more than make up for my lack of knowledge about Black history in years to come, coinciding with the appearance of my mentor, a subject we will delve into later in the book.

Even though I stated that in familiar surroundings I was protected, there were incidents that certainly seemed racially motivated. For instance, in second grade, a teacher picked me up by my neck with his bare hands as a form of discipline. When I was fourteen, I remember going to an indoor pool with my friends. Playing as youngsters do, the lifeguard told us to settle down. It seems that we were not quiet enough, so the lifeguard approached us again and, instead of disciplining all of us, singled me out and said, "You boy, get out of the pool." Now one may think that those incidents had nothing to do with racism, and I just may agree not being able to conclusively know that. However, it does seem strange that no other child had been picked up by the neck like I had been, or that despite others just as rambunctious as me, I was the one singled out. Whatever the reason may have been, it left an everlasting impression on me, and gave me the feeling that something was wrong with me.

There is a similar incident that happened years later, when I was on a senior high school trip. We were staying at a small town none of us had ever been before. Going to the community pool, I was quick to notice that I was the only dark kid there. The pools in Germany are built in such a way that before you reach the main pool, you have to wade through shallow standing water. I decided to step on the edge rather than go into the water, because the water was very cold.

A lifeguard saw that and told me to walk through the water. I didn't want to, and I didn't. I was not the only one who chose not to wade through the cold water.

Finally getting into the pool with my peers, we had fun playing around. We were doing nothing out of the ordinary, when the lifeguard approached us, pointed at me and said, "Get out of the pool." Words I had heard before. "Why?" some of my peers asked the lifeguard. "Because he is being too rowdy." Having no choice but to leave the pool, I thought that after a while the lifeguard would let me swim again. How wrong I was. He never let me in the pool again, despite the pleading of my peers. Here again, one can wonder whether this was just a coincidence of a lifeguard being in a bad mood that day, or were his actions racially motivated to keep me out of the pool. As ridiculous as it may sound, I felt that the reason I was not let in anymore was because I would dirty the pool.

I Am Not Ugly

I was always under the impression that my peers in high school didn't find me appealing. It was not until after I graduated high school in 1979 that I would find out that indeed many of the girls in my class thought I was attractive. What boosted my self-esteem was when a classmate of mine, Iris, told me the following story during a visit to Germany in 1983. I had invited her over to my house for tutoring, because she happened to be the smartest student in school; but I can assure you, tutoring was the last thing on my mind. "Remember that day when I came over to your house to tutor you, and I told you that my mother may have an issue with you being Black? You got so mad, and we had a terrible argument. Remember that?" "Yes, so what?" "Well, what I really was trying to do was to ask you if I could be your girlfriend." What a bombshell. I was stunned. She continued, "I was so nervous asking you, and the fear of what my mother would think about you being my boyfriend did not help. So I jumbled my words. I am so sorry; I never meant to hurt you. It was not the way I had hoped it would go."

Let me tell you, even though many years had passed, it made me feel great. Finally, I had confirmation that I was accepted by my peers. It was society that did not accept me, or should I say, it was society that did not accept the union between their white daughters and a black young man. It has been my experience that it is not so much individuals themselves, but society at large that puts this pressure on individuals to conform to society's standards. What made me feel even better was when she told me that many girls in high school thought I was cute, and many of them wished they could have dated me. They, however, did not dare to approach me because of society's racist guidelines, as the following account will illustrate.

I don't recall how or when I met this cute girl with red hair, but I ended up at a dance with her, and we had a good time. She invited me to her home one day, and I accepted. We walked into her house, and passing her parents, I said hello to them. The look on their faces was shocking, even for me. Talk about feeling uncomfortable and out of place. That is an understatement. And I could see how uncomfortable she was, too. You know the saying, 'If looks could kill?' Well, I would have dropped dead instantly. It was absolutely clear that her parents detested me being with their daughter. Suffice it to say, I never saw her again.

My Soccer Family

At the age of fourteen, I was recruited by a rival soccer team. The team was promoted to play in the *Verbandsliga*, which was the highest youth league in Germany. Playing for those two years at that level cemented my status in my town and region even more. Being naïve to racism, I never thought I had experienced it on the field. It was my teammates who corrected me on that subject. They informed me that there were times when players from the other team called me Neger or Schwarzer (German equivalent to Nigger), but rather than letting me know, they took care of it themselves. That explains the infractions taking place on the field for no apparent reason.

Though I played on many teams, without a doubt, this particular team was my favorite, simply because we were like a family. It felt like a family, because we would do many things together. We would meet to watch the men's team play, and afterwards would socialize. When we could not watch the men's team play, we would meet in town to go bowling or to the movies. That camaraderie transferred onto the playing field. I felt protected, and I was protected by them. One for all, all for one. As you can probably imagine, it was an environment that I loved to be in. I will forever be thankful for my teammates.

France

Only on one occasion did race play a role with my teammates; however, there was never any malicious intent. It was simply an innocent mistake. The town where I am from has a sister city in France, Antibes. We were invited to play soccer against a team there, and the *Fussball Verein* took a youth and a men's team to France. We, the boys, played our game in the morning, while the men's team played in the afternoon. I remember this game with much pleasure, because even though after being on the field only 15 minutes and already being down by two goals, we turned the game around and won. I had so much fun playing that game, and it must have shown, because I was invited to play for the men's team in the afternoon. (The only one, I may add!) I was 16 at the time, and technically not even allowed to play for the men's team. Of course, it was an honor for me to be invited to play. What a feeling to walk into the locker room and be among the players of the men's team.

In the second half, I entered the game. It was so overwhelming; I don't remember much of the game today. Just before I entered the game, my teammates started chanting *"Kun-ta Kin-te, Kun-ta Kin-te!"* The TV series *Roots* had just aired in Germany, and was very popular. Everybody knew who Kunta Kinte was. I enjoyed the chanting, because I knew my peers were cheering me on.

Later that evening, a teammate told me that the President of the club had called a meeting without my knowledge. In that meeting, my teammate said, "Man, he tore into us. He was so mad because we chanted Kunta Kinte. He made it clear that we were never to call you by that name again." *How amusing*, I thought. I never took it any other way, just as encouragement. I knew my teammates meant no harm or disrespect, and it was great to know that I was protected in that manner. Nonetheless, the status and respect I enjoyed in my town and region unfortunately did not transfer outside of my familiar surroundings. Outside those surroundings, I was just another black kid who was not welcome.

Great Summer

In 1978, I spent the summer with my cousin Eddie. We had a wonderful time together. In particular, I remember a field trip we took with a youth group. To this day, it ranks as my all-time favorite trip, ever. I won't even attempt to put into words the happiness and joy I felt that day.

Besides going to see some caves and swimming at a lake, we went to see a well-known outdoor play in Bad Segeberg. The play was called *Winnetou and Old Shatterhand*. To make things even better, Eddie and I were able to spend the trip with two girls. It was the best summer I ever had, even though I was to experience how differently I was treated outside of familiar surroundings, as the two following stories will show.

The Bar

Eddie and I went to a pub to have a drink. He knew the bartender, since he frequented this particular bar quite often. "Johnny, why don't you go and order two beers, please." "Okay." I went to the bar to order the beers. "Two beers, please." The bartender looked at me and asked, "Who are you here with?" "I'm here with Eddie, my cousin." "Show me," he demanded. He walked with me to the table to see if

I was telling the truth. Upon seeing Eddie, he joyfully greeted Eddie. "Hello Eddie, what can I get you?" "Two beers, please." "Of course, right away." I was dumbfounded, to say the least.

At first I thought he believed me to be a GI. American soldiers did not have a good reputation in town, since many of them were known to cause major problems when they had a few German beers in them. However, I spoke native German, so should not have been mistaken for a GI for that reason alone. Furthermore, I had long hair, which was another reason I should have never been mistaken for a soldier, period. I now understand; Eddie was in familiar surroundings, known and respected, whereas I was not. Therefore, I was unknown, and disrespected.

The Club

Another memorable incident happened when Eddie and I went to a club one night. He was walking in front of me as we approached the entrance. He paid and walked in. When I got ready to pay, the bouncer said, "No, you can't come in." *What? You're kidding me.* The feeling of rejection was all too familiar, and instantly made me sad. However, before I could tell the man that my cousin had just walked in, a young woman next to him put her hand on mine and said, "He is coming in." The bouncer did not challenge her. I will never forget her kind act, just like I will never forget how wonderfully soothing her hand felt on mine. In the blink of an eye, she made me feel so comfortable, so loved and accepted.

While in the club, I really wanted to talk to this beautiful angel, and though Eddie encouraged me, I was too shy to approach her. *Go talk to her. She is right there!* But I just couldn't find the courage to talk to her. Sure, my shyness was a result of being rejected countless times, but there was another reason why I did not approach her. In the back of my mind, I was convinced that had I gotten the nerve to speak to her, nothing would have come of it anyway. I had been clearly warned by German society that I was not welcome to engage in a relationship with their (white) daughters. So why even try? Sad, but that is how I felt.

Disturbing News

Just having spent a wonderful summer, my mother had some disturbing news for me. "Johnny, we are moving to America next year." "Not me. I am not going. I don't know America and besides, all my friends and family are here. No way." With a no-nonsense kind of tone, she said, "You are going. Your life will better in America than here in Germany." *For whom*, I thought, *you or me?* "Plus, you are not even allowed to live here without me." As I was to find out later, that was not true, simply another one of her countless lies.

Contrary to what she told me, I could have easily stayed in Germany without her. Living with my grandmother was an option. My soccer club was eager to keep me and would've helped me get a job. I did not know that back then, but as life would eventually show, all happened for a reason.

The grip my mother had on me was too strong. I was just not strong enough to fight her, nor strong enough to assert my will and opinion about not moving to America. Eventually that would change.

Intro into American Culture

Once I had conceded, I made a decision to prepare myself better for living in the States. We had a couple of Army bases in town. I decided to make friends with the so-called 'dependents', the children of the soldiers stationed in Germany. I became friends with peers my age, and was introduced into the American culture by way of movies, sports, and music.

Not only that, but I started dating. Caroline would become my first American girlfriend. She was my age and biracial; her father Black, and her mother White. To my surprise, her mother was German. On occasion, her mother and I would converse in German, which seemed strange to Caroline and her siblings, because they did not speak German. Actually, it was I who was surprised. I assumed they could speak their own mother's language.

So happy was I to have a girlfriend, especially one who looked similar to me, that I spent as much time as possible with her. She would get home from school around three in the afternoon, because the dependents went to an American school about an hour away, and I would be waiting for her. Every day. What I did not realize was that I was smothering her. Our relationship became rocky, and inevitably, she broke up with me. I was devastated. Looking back, I understand that I left her no choice. I was just too overbearing. Poor Caroline; she never stood a chance.

That year helped me tremendously to get used to the American culture. Until then, America was only familiar to me through *Starsky and Hutch*, a very popular TV series in Germany. I even owned a pair of the same blue and white Adidas shoes Starsky wore in the show. Nonetheless, I was still overwhelmed when I did finally arrive in America. It took years to get used to the American way of life. I believe my reluctance to move to America made the transition much harder than it needed to be.

Arriving in America

The August after I graduated high school, in 1979, I left to go and live in America. It was not a happy day for me. The biggest issue for me was that I was going to America shortly before I turned eighteen. It was bitter celebrating my eighteenth birthday, a birthday that I had been looking forward to all my life, in a foreign country, without my friends. I never again celebrated birthdays the way I had before; at least not until many years later, when I would somewhat celebrate my birthday, again.

It may be difficult to understand that I felt this way, but what needs to be understood is that although I grew up in a country that would not accept me as an equal, it was the only country that I knew. It's not like I experienced only negative things. Of course not. I had my share of positive things happen, too. Unfortunately, the more I was rejected, the more I would do whatever I could to be accepted. It was a way of trying to fill the void I felt inside of me. It was a way to prove to myself that I was worthy, something I had been trying to prove to myself all my life.

I am not sure why I felt this void, or how to fill it. Why was I trying to prove to myself that I was worthy? Then I asked myself a simple but heartfelt question: did my mother really love me?

Did Mother Love Me?

Did my mother not love me? Was she ashamed of me? Did she reject me because the pressure by German society was so great that she could not handle it? I pondered those questions innumerable times. German society was clear about those questions: no, they did not love me. Yes, they were ashamed of me. Yes, they rejected me. I learned to live with that. C'est la vie!

Understandably, my low self-esteem was in big part due to the lack of acceptance in Germany. Unfortunately, adding to my dilemma was my mother's rejection of me. Dealing with society's rejection is one thing. Dealing with my mother's rejection is an entirely different matter. I vividly remember walking down the street with her as a teenager, grabbing her hand, and my mother shaking it loose so it would not draw attention to us. At times when I hugged her, she broke the embrace, because she seemed ashamed of me. How do you deal with rejection when it comes from your own mother? How do you process the unfathomable?

What's more, the memories of the beatings, the mental, emotional, and verbal abuse, and the confusion as a result, have left me believing that she did not love me. Knowing what I know about my mother, the fact that her image was extremely important to her, it would seem that I was taken care of and loved by her. Yes, she clothed and fed me, but what people didn't see was what happened

behind closed doors. They did not see the lack of comforting, nurturing and love.

Single German mothers already had a tough time in society, and
to compound the situation by adding a Black child to the equation
would seem to make life even more difficult. I would like to think that
maybe my mother chose to treat me this way because of the immense
pressure she felt from German society, not because she did not love
me. It's the lesser of the two evils. I have my doubts though, simply
because as I got older, she had countless opportunities to make up
for the past. She could have stopped the emotional, physical, and
mental abuse and treated me the way I deserved to be treated. That
never happened. Instead, she tried everything in her power to keep
her dominance over me.

Losing Control Over Me

As I got older, our relationship worsened. Whereas before our
arguments were reasonably minor, the arguments increased in inten-
sity and frequency. Her frustration and anger intensified as I stood my
ground, as she started to understand that she was losing control over
me. That, I believe, is one of the reason for the increased tension
between us. "I am your mother. I am always right," were statements
she often made. In her world, there was no room for any other opinion; certainly not mine.

To try to gain control, she resorted to ridiculing me, or using physical force. Unfortunately for her, controlling me by using physical force
soon ended. The last time I remember her trying to use physical in-
timidation was when I was fourteen years old. As it so often happened,
we were arguing about something trivial. Standing directly in front of
her, I disagreed with what she was saying. Her face turned beet red. I
could see her anger and frustration building. In spite of the warning
signs, I stood my ground, and did not give in. She hated that with a passion. Raising her hand to slap me, I caught it in midair, and looked her
sternly in the eyes. After a few seconds, I let go. It was the last time my

mother attempted to strike me. Surely, that added more to her frustration, because she realized the physical dominance over me was gone.

Finally, I believe that my mother never wanted to keep me. The only reason she kept me was to hurt my father as best she could. What I don't think she understood then is that by making that decision, she hurt all three of us. I am convinced that her decision, and her subsequent frustration and anger, were the reasons behind her appalling treatment of me.

Seeing My Father

A couple of weeks after arriving in the States, I called my father. He seemed happy to hear from me, and agreed to send for me, so I could spend some time with him. *Wow,* I thought, *I'm going to see my father again!* I was nervous, because it had been more than thirteen years since I last saw him. I was eager to talk to him. The pain of being abandoned by him still stung tremendously. So many questions went through my mind. He picked me up at the airport, and once I settled in, he allowed me the opportunity to speak about the past during the week I spent with him.

"Why did you leave me in Germany?" There it was; the question I had been waiting to ask my father for over thirteen years. "Son," he said, with a serious voice, "I wanted to take you with me, but when your mother said, '*Over my dead body,*' I knew there was nothing I could do. You should know that I wanted you." Though his answer sounded plausible, I still had my doubts. I wished that his efforts of fighting for me would have been stronger, more visible. I asked him many more questions. There were many things that he agreed with, and quite a few things that he told me were not correct. It was refreshing to get clarification on many of the things my mother told me, and it was good to finally hear the other side of the story, intuitively feeling that much of what my mother told me were lies.

When I related some of my father's stories to Tante Toni, she confirmed the information. *So he was correct.* It was a confirmation of what I had always felt. My father was not the bad guy my mother had me believe. This was very important to me. At least now I knew that I was not rejected by him. It certainly helped improve my self-worth. I also understood that all the hateful feelings that I received from my mother were her problem, not mine. It is clear to me, that she never forgave herself for having a child with a black man.

This begs the question, a question that had been bothering me for the longest time: why did she get involved with my father, a black man, to begin with? It is a question that, unfortunately, will forever stay unanswered.

Finding Acceptance

Living in the States, I thought that my acceptance level would rise, and it did; but all was not groovy though. I did on occasion meet black people who had a problem with the fact that I was half white. To them, I was not black enough. At least the acceptance level here in America was higher than in Germany. In Germany, I am a *Neger*. In America, I am a *Half-breed*. Go figure.

One pleasant surprise was the reaction I received from black girls. At times, I felt like a star at a rock concert, with girls screaming when they saw me. It took some getting used to, something I really did not mind doing though. Undoubtedly, that raised my self-esteem, and to finally find acceptance and be liked for what I looked like, was an incredible feeling.

University

In 1981, my mother and stepfather went back to live in Germany. I was recruited to play soccer for Campbell University. The day my parents dropped me off at Campbell is deeply imprinted in my mind. After almost twenty years of living with my mother, I was going to finally be free. Saying goodbye in the parking lot seemed very difficult for her, because she cried pretty hard. I, on the other hand, did not shed a single tear. Seeing her drive off, a weight lifted off of me. I was elated. The feeling of being free was incredible. To this day, I am not sure why she cried. Her behavior seemed hypocritical to me.

Being on my own for the very first time was something I had to get used to. Even though I was happy to be away from my mother, the first few days were lonely for me. The first person I befriended was one of the few black students who attended the university. She was a very kindhearted soul, showing me around, and helping me get situated on campus. Her kindness will never be forgotten.

Sadly, once I got in with the soccer team, I stopped hanging out with her. One could say that practice and time with the team did not allow me to spend much time with her, but that is not quite the truth. It seems that though I yearned to be with people who looked more like me, I was more comfortable among white people.

A year later, I was confronted by another black female student who accused me of avoiding black people. *Nonsense*, I thought. I did not understand then what she meant. I do now. She was right, but it was not because I didn't want to; it was that I was seeking an environment that I was familiar with. You can say that I was conditioned to hang out with white people and avoid people of color. When I think back at the continuous barrage of negative images about black people that my mother bombarded me with, being conditioned to dislike black people makes sense. What I did not realize at that moment was that I disliked myself. It would take me years to break out of that conditioning.

Martha

It was at Campbell that I, for the first time, heard that white girls found me attractive (the story with my classmate happened later). It was at a party my sophomore year, and I was sitting next to this cute girl Martha. We got into a conversation about dating, when all of a sudden she paid me a compliment. "You know John, you are really good-looking." Caught off guard, I responded in a manner of disbelief, "What, are you kidding?" "No, I am not kidding. Many of my friends agree with me." That was the very first time I had heard that white girls were attracted to me. To put into words the relief that I felt when I heard the compliment is impossible. My own white mother made me feel undesirable, and now I was hearing that someone else who is white thinks I am okay. Finally to be acknowledged for part of my heritage that had been shunned all my life was an immense feeling. *Maybe there is light at the end of the tunnel,* I thought.

Going Back Home

Having completed my freshman year, I was able to visit home again. Finally! It had been almost three years since I'd left Germany. The excitement I felt upon returning home was indescribable. The entire trip on the plane was surreal. My mother and stepfather picked me up from the airport. Walking around on German ground, seeing German cars and signs, was unreal to me. Even driving down the famous Autobahn, I was in a trance, and could not believe I was finally home again.

My parents had moved to Worms, a city I was unfamiliar with. Upon arriving at their home, I still did not believe that I was in Germany, so I asked my mother to visit Tante Gina and Tante Toni, who were living about an hour from Worms. Arriving at my Tantes' house, it finally sunk in; I was really in Germany. Tante Gina was living on the first floor with her children, and Tante Toni was living on the third floor with hers.

My favorite cousin was Eddie. As previously stated, we formed a strong bond early on. He was my idol. Whenever I was in his company, I felt I was invincible. Undoubtedly, my self-esteem was boosted when I was around him. Not only was I in great company, but on top of that, I had a role model. So understandably, he was the one I was most excited to see.

After a quick hello to Tante Gina and her kids, I ran upstairs to see

Eddie. Knowing the love we had for each other, I couldn't wait to see him again. I rang the doorbell, and he opened the door. Ready to hug him, he stood at the door, just looking at me and asked in a very non-chalant way, "Yeah, what do you want?" I was totally caught off-guard by his greeting. Shocked, hurt and so disappointed, I nevertheless decided to visit with him. The subsequent conversation, however, was forced, and void of any emotions. After a short while I left, wondering what the reason was for his behavior. Days later, I was to find out, but it did nothing to mend our relationship. It would never be the same again.

Believing that I had returned from the States a conceited person was the reason he treated me coldly. My mother's joy in sharing newspaper articles I was featured in had not been well-received. Certainly, my mother was pleased that I was attending a university and was a star soccer player. Her image as a good mother was extremely important to her; and my doing so well just raised her image. Rather than being happy for me though, Eddie decided to use it against me. Perplexed by his behavior, I was talking on the phone with Eddie one day when Tante Toni said to him, "Johnny is not conceited. He is the same old Johnny." Too late. Damage done.

What bothered me back then was the fact that he did not give me a chance to reintroduce myself, to find out for himself that I had not changed. Years later, it led me to a different conclusion of why Eddie acted the way he did. Eddie is also biracial. His father is Black and his mother, my aunt, White. Unlike me, he has never met his father. Eddie is pro-American, and he would often have these heated debates with a friend over who was the real superpower: the United States or Russia? It is my belief that Eddie's behavior was a result of jealousy. Instead of him, it was me who was living in the States, and me who had met my father.

Though Eddie had the total support of his mother, I know how he was treated by German society. He faced racism and discrimination just like I did, and to find some level of acceptance, he had to prove himself daily. The pressure of having to do this was immense, and surely had profound implications for him in the future. I cannot speak for him, so I don't know exactly how he handled this adversity, but I am convinced that it left a mark on him. This is why I conclude his strange behavior towards me was caused by the jealousy of me having escaped Germany.

Now, I considered the possibility of being wrong; however, my theory of him being jealous was confirmed many years later by no other than his own mother. It is also why I am not mad at Eddie. I'm just immensely saddened that our relationship is broken. Having been more of a brother to me than a cousin, I wish him nothing but the best. I have much love for him.

As I mentioned above, Eddie enjoyed the full support of his mother. My mother did not think much of Eddie, and spoke negatively about him. It was a behavior I did not understand back then, especially since Eddie had never done anything to disrespect her. Today, I know why she acted that way. You see, Eddie was the proverbial Black, which meant in her world, he was no good. I so much envied Eddie back then, as I do now, for having a mother who supported, loved, and above all else, accepted him for who he was. I commend Tante Toni tremendously for standing by her son, understanding that life for her was also not easy.

Staying at Tante Gina's Place

Tante Gina's husband, who was American, had just died, so she and her kids went to America to visit family. She offered to let me stay in her apartment, and I accepted. Not having to spend the summer at my mother's place was great. It was the summer of 1982, and the soccer World Cup was being played in Spain. I was extremely excited, because it was an extra incentive to train hard, and to be in shape for the upcoming season at Campbell. Believe me, by the end of the summer, I was in shape; probably the best shape I have ever been in my life. Out of my familiar surroundings, I received different treatment from the people in town though. They did not know me, so to them, I was a stranger—a black stranger.

Jenny's Parents

I had known Jenny since the second grade, and whenever I came to town, we got together. We were walking into town one day when a car pulled up, and her parents got out. Immediately, her mother and father yelled at her. Well, her mother was more screaming than yelling. Jenny's mother grabbed her, and pulled her into the car. Her father stood in front of me, berating me, and calling me all kinds of nasty names. His next move was unexpected. He slapped me. Shocked, I stood frozen. Unbelievable; I was assaulted in broad daylight! What made me very angry though was that I did not protect or defend myself. Having been intimidated by life's circumstances was the reason for my lack of defense. I did not dare to cause any trouble, even if it was in my own defense. In time, I would learn to handle life better.

What stands out most in my mind, was the anger and hatred I saw in the faces of Jenny's parents. I could also see the fear and shame in their eyes. The fear of their daughter getting involved with a Schwarzer, and God forbid, having a child; and the shame of how they would be perceived in town. There was no mistake; I was not welcome in their town.

What I was to soon find out was that even in my own hometown, I was now a stranger.

Not My Home Anymore

On a visit to my hometown, Schwäbisch Gmünd, Bernd, a close friend of mine and I went to a restaurant for dinner. We had grown up together, and knew each other well. Sitting at dinner talking about old times, he asked me an interesting question. "Johnny, why are you choosing to live in America, when Germany is your home?" Surprised, I answered, "Because in America, life is easier for me, since I am Black. It would be much harder here." *This is my mother's opinion. I don't really believe it*, is what I wanted to tell him, but didn't.

"Nonsense. That's bull." It had not escaped me that since we had arrived at the restaurant, people had been staring at us. Clearly, these people did not appreciate the fact that I was sitting here having dinner with my friend. The expressions on their faces unmistakably read: you are not welcome here. "Look behind you at the people over there please, and tell me what you see." He did not hide that he was looking, and the people were not hiding their expressions, either.

As he turned towards me again, I could see tears running down his face. It was a moment of profound sadness for him, and the pain was written all over his face. "Johnny," he said, crying, "had I not seen this with my own eyes, I would never have believed you. You are like a brother to me, and my family treats you like one of our own. I am so ashamed." He understood.

The reason for the people's reaction is explained easily. Before, when I was living in town, I was well-known; I was now a stranger to them. I had been away from home long enough for them to have forgotten who I was. To people now, I was just another black man who did not belong. As difficult as it was for me to believe, what was once my home, was not my home, anymore.

Schoko

Returning to Campbell after an eventful summer, I entered my sophomore year. Shortly afterward, I met Schoko, a freshman student who would become my first serious girlfriend. She was a beautiful, biracial woman. Her mother was Japanese, and her father White. I was very taken by her from the get-go. Interestingly, it took a little time to get through to her. I got the message early on that she was hesitant to get involved with me because of my race. *Here we go again,* I thought. *Strange, how is that possible? She is a minority just like me.* Well, come to find out, it was her parents who were prejudiced, especially her mother.

This was astonishing to me. How can a minority be prejudiced against another minority? Equally astonishing was the fact that her father claimed a black man as his best friend. Whatever the dynamics were in that home, it surely had a great effect on her. It was not until I was well into my journey of self-discovery that I would understand that minorities unfortunately show prejudice among themselves. However, what became obvious was that whenever Black was in the mix, racism showed its ugliest side. More about that later.

Schoko later told me that she was taken by me immediately, but was scared. I understood all too well, since I had lived with those experiences my entire life. To her credit, she overcame her fear, and we enjoyed a wonderful relationship for the next couple of years. Towards the end of my senior year, our relationship was put under immense stress because of my dream of becoming a professional soccer player in Germany.

Leaving the Creek

After I graduated college in 1985, I left for Germany. She cried a great deal. "Please don't go. I love you so much." It did not help that I was her first love. Talk about being torn; torn between the woman you love, and your dream. "Schoko, I too love you so much, but I have to go. I need to follow my dream. We will be in touch, and hopefully see each other very soon."

My mother lived in a beautiful one-bedroom apartment. Sleeping on the couch was not a problem for me. I lived there from May through September. I'm not quite sure how my mother could afford this apartment because, according to her, she barely had money, a detail that will play a curious role in a minute. Complaining about not having enough food, she often went to Oma to eat. As much as she could, she made me feel uncomfortable.

Fortunately, I quickly found a team to play on. Nonetheless, our relationship was very tense during my stay with her, and it was obvious that she did not want me there. In September, for various personal reasons, I brought up the issue of possibly going back to the States. When I approached my mother about going back to

America, she was suddenly very supportive. So supportive, believe it or not, that she came up with the money for my plane ticket, despite claiming that she barely had enough money to survive. The message was unmistakable: I don't want you here. So much for motherly love. And though her rejection was not new, it was still difficult to deal with.

Returning to the Creek

Even though I was gone only four months, my relationship with Schoko was never the same again. She would later admit that when I left, it had scared her immensely. Not wanting to put herself in this kind of situation again, she guarded herself. We dated off and on before she left to pursue a career out of state. Years later, she told me that she always thought we would get married. There was no doubt in her mind. Yeah, I could see that. However, it was not meant to be.

I hold Schoko in the highest regard. She will always occupy a special corner of my heart, and I wish her all the best that life has to offer.

Finding Family—Dave

In 1986, Oma died. I was devastated. I received a call from my mother late one night. When I answered the phone, she could barely speak, which scared me. Finally, she got out the words that Oma had died. I was numb. Here I was, three thousand miles away from home, without my family. Luckily, something wonderful was about to happen. If I thought I was without family, I was to be corrected by one of the most emotional and profound incidents of my life.

The next day, I went to see my French Professor, Dr. Steegar. We had taken a liking to one another, and I felt comfortable around him. Unbeknownst to me, he was about to show me what being accepted and loved was all about. As I walked into his office, I wanted to tell him about Oma. Before I could utter a single word, I started crying. He immediately got up, guided me to a chair and closed the door.

Then he hugged me and let me cry. No words were spoken. He just held me. This simply gesture of love he allowed me to feel still brings tears to my eyes, even when I think about it today. It is a moment too profound to put into words, and it is a moment that is deeply embedded in my heart.

Finally, I was able to tell him what happened. His words were soothing and comforting. "You know John, my grandmother passed away while I was in Europe. So I know how you feel. I was also close to her." Hearing that he had been through a very similar situation helped calm me down, and I was able to collect my feelings and thoughts. If there ever was a kind gesture in my life that reassured me that I was loved and accepted, this was it. I forever will be thankful for the way he handled the situation. It cemented our relationship, and Dave has been in my life ever since.

Leaving North Carolina

I decided to visit my mother for Christmas the same year Oma died. I had to say goodbye to Oma, and before seeing my mother, I had a friend take me by the cemetery to visit Oma's grave. I had found this beautiful card, before I left North Carolina, that I translated into German. I put the card on the grave, which I now regret. I so wish I would have kept the card, since the words in it were not only beautiful and profound, but also described her perfectly. However, I realize the reason I left the card on the grave was so that I could begin healing.

Tired of living in North Carolina, I made a decision to either move permanently to Germany, or to Los Angeles, California. Intuitively, I knew that I was going to move to California, and told my mother that I was thinking about moving to Los Angeles. My father had been living there for many years, and I was hoping that he would help me get started.

"Mama, I am thinking about moving to Los Angeles, and will ask my father if I can stay with him until I can make it on my own." "What? Absolutely not." She must have thought that she was speaking to a child, believing she had a say in this decision. "He abandoned you, and never did anything for you. Why would you want to live with him?" "The past is the past. I can't change that," I countered. Realizing that she was unable to talk me out of moving to L.A., she switched gears. "Well, then let him make up for the past and pay for everything you need. He owes you that and more." "No, I only want him to help me get on my feet. That's all." I was not surprised at my mother's anger and frustration about hearing that I was moving to my father, because it was her biggest fear that I would find out about what really happened back then.

Moving to Los Angeles

Though I did not know my father well, I asked him if I could stay with him. He agreed. I spent the next 16 months living at his house. We bonded well, and had a great time. When I moved in, my father said, "Though it might be too late to raise you, it is not too late to be good friends." "Sounds great," I agreed. That is exactly how our relationship was. We were more like friends than father and son.

I enjoyed being around him. He used to work for a moving company, and quite often would take a side job on weekends. I would often help him. It was physical work, but after a good day's work, I looked forward to having dinner or even a beer with him.

Shortly after I moved in with my father, I was hired at a gym as a fitness instructor. A few weeks after working at the gym, I started dating a woman, who would become my girlfriend. Interestingly enough, she was also biracial, although I was not aware of it then. Not that it mattered, but it's interesting, nevertheless. Her father was Irish-American, and her mother Mexican. Parallel to the situation with Schoko, her mother did not care for me, either.

Christmas 1987

My mother's dislike for me did not lessen even as I got older, nor when in the company of others. I had moved to California in March of 1987. Deciding to go back to Germany for Christmas, I brought my neighbor friend John-John along for the trip. My mother was living in the family house with her sister, and I was excited to spend Christmas there. Upon my arrival, my mother was furious to see that I had brought my friend to stay with us. I was confused, especially since she told me that this was also my house. Furthermore, there was enough room, and we were going to pay for the food.

Before I left California, I asked my father if it would be okay if I bought a plane ticket for my mother and have her come and visit me in California. He agreed, so I bought, as a Christmas gift, a plane ticket for her. John-John wanted to give my mother a gift also, so we bought her some winter boots that she had said she wanted. On Christmas Eve, we presented the gifts to my mother, telling her one gift was from me, and the other from John-John.

"What's this?" she said, when she saw the ticket. "It's an airline ticket to California. I want you to come for a visit." Not even a thank you; just all kinds of excuses to why she could not go to California. "I can't leave at this time. I have things to do." *Strange*, I thought. *She is not working, so has enough time for a visit.* "Mama, this is an open-ended plane ticket. You can come whenever you are ready," I said, thinking that there was no way for her to get out of this one. Wrong. She was adamant that there wasn't any way she could take the time for a visit. In other words: *I will never come for a visit.*

She then opened the other gift, and when she saw the boots, she went into a tirade. "These are not the boots I wanted!" *Interesting; those are the ones you showed us when we were in town.* "They're cheap and not even my size." "That's okay Mama, you can exchange them for any boots you want." Even though I kind of anticipated her reaction, I was still confused and majorly embarrassed. Embarrassed not only for me, but especially for my friend John.

There are many more dreadful incidences that happened on that visit, but I will end by saying that even in my twenties, my mother still treated me the way she always had: with disdain.

Moving Back to Germany

Having spent the last sixteen months in Los Angeles was fantastic. Yet, I still felt the need to fill one particular void. Obviously, I had not healed from missing out on playing soccer in Germany the way I had always dreamed of doing. Wanting to play soccer while I was still in top physical shape, I made the decision to leave Los Angeles and spend a few years in Germany. Though some of my friends thought I was crazy to leave sunny California to live in rainy Germany, I had made up my mind. Fortunately, my best friend Coco supported me unconditionally, like always. He simply said, "Johnny, of course you are going to stay with me until you can get your own place." How wonderful to have his support, and I would need it, because I had no idea what an adventure I was about to step into.

In July of 1988, I left for Germany, and my girlfriend followed me three months later. The plan was to live there a few years, and then go back to California; but instead of staying a few years, I stayed only six months. As I was soon to discover, it was during those six months that my life would change forever.

Self-Discovery Journey Begins

Growing up, I always believed I was treated well by my mother. I had no reason to believe otherwise. One day, my girlfriend asked me, "Why are you letting your mother treat you so badly?" I was shocked at that accusation, and in disbelief. "What are you talking about? There is nothing wrong with the way she treats me!" I exclaimed. Though I did not believe her, it still bothered me for some reason. So to clarify these accusations, I asked my best friend, "Coco, tell me, do you ever remember my mother treating me badly?" *If anyone knows, he does,* I thought.

So that you will understand why Coco's opinion meant so much to me, an explanation is in order. Coco and I have been friends (no, more like brothers) for more than forty years. We grew up living only a couple of blocks from each other, and shared many great times together. He has been there for me through thick and thin. It's hard to describe the bond that we share between us, but suffice it to say: no words need to be spoken to know how the other feels.

Interestingly, I would spend many nights sleeping at his house, but never, not once, did he spend a night at my house. Whenever I would go to his house, his mother would *always* greet me with hugs and kisses, which made me feel so loved and welcome. She was more like a mother to me than my own mother ever was.

There are way too many wonderful things Coco did for me to share with you, reader, at this point in time; but know that he is the brother I never had. I cherish the day we became friends, as I continue to cherish the tremendous positive effect he has had, and continues to have, in my life. So you see, when I asked him whether he ever remembered my mother treating me badly, his answer affected me profoundly.

What he said next shocked me to my core. "Johnny," he hesitantly said, "there were times when I thought the way she treated you was not okay." *Boom!* What just happened? *Did he just say what I thought he said?* I fell into an abyss and was free falling with no end in sight. Knowing Coco very well, I knew that it was extremely difficult for him to admit this. His words crushed me, especially since I knew how to read between the lines. He was trying to be as tactful with his words as he could, but what he really said was: *yes, your mother treated you badly!* Stunned, I had nothing to say to him.

I thank my 'brother' Coco, for having the courage for being so honest with me. Because of him, I started my journey of self-discovery at that very moment. It was the beginning of a very profound and intense journey that lasted for more than a decade. However, without his courage and honesty, I would probably still live the illusion that my mother loved and respected me. Words will never be able to express my gratitude for Coco!

Now I started to understand. Playing back memories of my upbringing, the memories of the countless beatings and arguments. The memories of my mother escaping my hugs or letting go of my hand when I was trying to hold hers; all these memories started to make sense. My mother did not like the fact that I was part Black. She did not accept me as a biracial person. Truth told, my mother did not accept me as her son.

I had been fighting for acceptance all my life with German society, and I knew I had lost that battle. But to realize that I had lost the battle of acceptance with my mother was crushing. Yet, as bad as all this sounds, it had a wonderful benefit. It eventually allowed me to feel better about my past and myself. If I hadn't been told the truth, I may not ever have been able to correct my path in life. The fact that I listened meant that I was ready to hear the truth. It was time. Please know, it is not always easy to hear the truth, especially if it's unpleasant. And boy was it unpleasant for me! The only safe world I had known, crumbled. **It crumbled because it was an illusion**. It was a lie I had lived. So thankfully, I became disillusioned. Being disillusioned is a good thing, because it shatters an illusion. That, my friends, was the best thing that could have happened to me, at that time.

Before going back to California, I got married. Despite the tension with my mother, I was adamant that she would attend the wedding; however, my mother refused. I don't remember how many attempts I made trying to talk her into coming to the wedding, but finally I was able to persuade her to join us. All through the wedding though, it was clear that she was uncomfortable. I, nevertheless, was glad that she was in attendance, and after the ceremony, I hugged her. As happy as I was hugging her, she was uncomfortable because when I hugged her, she pushed me away. Fortunately for me that day, my happiness overpowered her rejection...but I still felt the pain.

Back in Los Angeles

Back in Los Angeles again, I was able to get a job at the same fitness studio I had worked at before. Shortly thereafter, I became friends with Glodean, who was a member at the gym. At the time I met her, I had no idea who she was. There were very few Blacks at that gym, and it surprised me even more when she said that she had been a member there for a while. Well, I inevitably found out that she was not only the wife of a world-renowned singer, but also a wonderful singer in her own right. It was her husband, however, who would become my greatest teacher and mentor.

The gym ended up closing down, which was actually a blessing in disguise, since I had been playing with the thought of having my own fitness business. "How about training me at my house?" Glodean asked me one day. "Fantastic!" I responded. I had my first student, and my fitness business was started. We would meet at her house three times a week to train.

Having developed a great relationship with Glodean, I shared a very personal thought with her one day. "Glo," as she liked to be called, "I need to ask you something. Even though I am secure and confident about myself, there is a part of me that just does not know where I belong." "I am not the one to talk to. You need to speak to Barry." "Talk to Barry, really?" I said hesitantly. "Yes, really," was her simple response.

I had run into Barry White on occasion at the house, but other than saying hello, we didn't talk. So one day, with Glodean's encouragement, I asked him if he could spare a couple of minutes so I could talk to him about a personal issue. He agreed, not knowing that this conversation, which was to last only a couple of minutes, would lead to countless conversations, lasting hours on end at times.

My Mentor

Our first meeting took place by the pool. I was silent and too intimidated to start the conversation. Barry finally said, "You're going to have to start, because I can't read your mind." The ice was broken. Feeling more comfortable, I repeated the same thought I had shared with Glodean. What came next influenced me tremendously then, as it still does to this day. The journey of self-discovery would jump into an even higher gear. "You are Black," is the first thing he said.

"That is what people see first, and is to be respected." He then went on to speak so highly of black people and their great accomplishments, that I immediately felt a boost in confidence. Though I do not consider myself Black today, Barry's claim that I was Black was the push that was needed for me to jump into a higher gear regarding my self-discovery.

Knowing little about my Black heritage, I decided to get a better understanding of who I was, and immersed myself into Black history. Having learned a lot about European history in school, but very little about Black history, I naturally wanted to know about the other half of my heritage. The information I found was overwhelming. Until then, I had no idea that there was a positive side to black people. That may sound ridiculous, but it is true. There isn't much Black history taught in schools in America. There is virtually no information about Black history in schools in Germany.

Though angry at first after reading about the racism and discrimination Black people endured, I was pleased to read about the many great accomplishments of not only Black people, but of other people of color as well. For instance, it was incredible to read about the great civilizations of Egypt. It was fantastic to find out a Black man, Daniel H. Williams, performed the first-ever open-heart surgery on July 9, 1893. It was fabulous to read that Asians invented the compass, or that Hispanics improved the submarine by adding a steam generator, which allowed a submarine to submerge for seven hours instead of just two.

Yes, there are different people of color on this globe, but we are all from the same home; and ultimately, we all have a story to tell.

My research did a great deal to help me understand myself better and eventually, I accepted myself as a biracial person. I felt secure enough to appreciate and acknowledge my racial heritage, and the unique aspects of all cultures.

Barry was gracious enough to share many hours with me, imparting great knowledge. I had finally found a male role model. I remember one evening while I was at his home, he took me outside to the pool. "John, whenever I'm not here, come over and use the pool; stay at the house and make yourself feel at home." What a wonderful gesture. He even took time out of his busy schedule to come to my wedding reception. "Thank you so much for coming, B." His response filled me with great pride. "The only reason why I am here John, is because of you." Later I would take a picture with Barry and my father. "Come on John," he said to my father, "let's take a picture with our son." Wow, talk about feeling accepted, talk about being loved!

I share this with you to help you understand how great it felt to finally receive a great amount of love for being who I am, and for finally having the male role model I so yearned for all my life! I had developed so much love and respect for Barry that it was confusing me. At one point, I felt guilty because the impact Barry had on my life was much greater than my father's. "It's okay to feel this way. Your father was not supposed to raise you. You had to experience what you did to be able to go on doing what you are meant to do in life." Powerful words.

"John, you and I are the same. The only difference is that I am older than you. I will always have more life experience, but eventually you will get where I am." These were empowering words. "Barry, why do you spend so much time having these conversations with me?" He looked into my eyes and said, "Because you listen, you pay attention. I believe when the student is ready, the teacher will appear." Well, did the teacher ever appear!

There were countless situations and talks we shared, too many to write down. Suffice it to say though, the impact Barry made on my life is still felt to this very day, and it will accompany me throughout my life. I realize that it was Barry who was supposed to be my mentor, not my father. For this reason, I am okay with my father not raising me. Had my father raised me, my life surely would be different, and I probably would not be writing these lines right now.

As a little side note, Barry and his crew would always call one another Doc. I would've loved to have been able to share with him the day I became a doctor. But I know he is watching, and knows.

The Beginning of the End

It was in February of 1992 that I received the news that I was about to become a father. So I decided to fly to Germany and tell my mother that she was going to be a grandmother. After all, I was her only child; and naturally, bringing her this joyful news was a big deal for me. It was also a wonderful opportunity to see Coco, in addition to visiting with Barry, who was on the European part of his world tour.

The day after arriving from California, I invited my mother for lunch. True to her personality, she complained about life and whatever else she could complain about. Listening patiently, I waited for the opportunity to give her the wonderful news. Not able to hold back anymore, I burst out, "Mama, you are going to be an Oma!" Silence. As if having to pick her next words carefully, she said, "I hope your child does not treat you as badly as you treated me." Bam! *You're kidding me? I've come six thousand miles to bring you great news, and you insult me?* I screamed in my head. Not wanting to argue, I did not show my true feelings. We finished lunch, and I took her home. If I thought that her comment over lunch was shocking, it was about to reach a level of '*this is unbelievable.*'

When it was time for me to leave Germany, I called her and said I was coming to say goodbye. Her next words are the most shocking words I ever heard my mother say to me, and I hear them as clearly today as I did back then. Devoid of any emotion, she coldly said, "Let's not play around anymore; I don't ever want to have anything to do with you anymore, ever." Unbelievable! I was stunned. It was the beginning of the end of our relationship; I just did not realize it yet. For a while I kept in touch with her, but eventually I let go.

I cannot tell you how many times I've asked myself why she would say such a thing. Her claim that I treated her badly is groundless, simply untrue. Was I a perfect son? Certainly not. But I can tell you that I never disrespected my mother to the extent that she claimed I did. It didn't make sense, because I was too intimidated and scared of her. I did not deserve to hear those words. It was clear to me that it was one more rejection, added to the countless other times I was rejected by her. I believe the reason I wasn't shattered when my mother told me she never wanted to have anything to do with me, was that the joy and happiness of the impending birth of my first child numbed the shock of her words. Nonetheless, I was deeply hurt!

Lisa

Due to personal issues, my first marriage did not work out. One always wonders what could have been done to change things, to solve the issues and save the relationship, but in the end, the conclusion is simply: it was meant to be this way.

Years after my marriage ended, I met Lisa. She is Dutch-Indonesian. For the third time in my life, I entered into a long-term relationship with a woman of biracial descent. At the beginning, Lisa told me that she was worried about having Black children. Even to her, I was Black, rather than biracial. What's more, according to Lisa, some members of her family were prejudiced against Blacks. *Are we ever going to get away from these racial issues?* To Lisa's credit, it did not deter her, and we got married three years later.

We each brought a child into our relationship; her son Anthony, whom I would eventually adopt, and my son Tahi. Together we have three children: Tiana, John, and Nico. In Lisa, I met a woman who treats children the way they should be treated. She is extremely loving and nurturing. Our children could not have asked for a better mother. Of course, we have different methods of how we raise our children, and sometimes that causes problems. That is only natural. What I am most impressed with is that, like me, she understands how important it is to give our children the love and support they need. As you know, I did without the love, comfort, and nurturing from my own mother, so recognize when it is lacking or present. With Lisa, it is definitely present.

It is even more important because our children are naturally of multiracial descent. As I have been maintaining, racism is alive today. Case in point, our children experience racism in school. Just the other day, John came home complaining that he is being called 'Nigger.' Not only that, they also talk negatively about us, his parents. Tiana, our beautiful daughter, is also confronted with racial overtones in school. Nico, our youngest, is still oblivious of society's issues with race. Unfortunately, I fear it will change, even for him.

From time to time, the subject of race finds its way to the dinner table. We eat dinner together every night, and I am amazed to hear that racism is so prevalent in schools today; that it is still widespread in society. Though we discuss these topics, mostly we instill confidence in our children, leading by example. Meaning, the way Lisa and I treat and talk about people of all races, helps our children to see that all people are to be treated with respect. Most of all, we teach our children to respect themselves. They have been to Germany, and are always visiting with either side of our family, being exposed to the Dutch, Indonesian, and Black cultures continuously.

As I continue speaking around the world, Lisa and the children will be introduced to other cultures. We hope it will enhance their tolerance, understanding and love for all people.

Mother Pays Us a Visit

I had not seen my mother for many years, and had it not been for a request by her, I most likely would not have ever seen her again. Shortly after my son, John-John, was born in January of 2000, I received a call form my mother informing me that she was coming to the States to visit a friend of hers in Texas. She told me that her friends in Germany didn't even know that she had grandchildren, and not being one to be embarrassed (worried about her image), she asked if she could come and visit us. Of course I knew the real reason why she was coming, though Lisa was hoping and wishing that she was coming to see us because she wanted to, and not because she needed to get pictures of her grandchildren.

The plan was for her to stay one month. Two weeks into her visit, I had a golden opportunity to talk to her without interruption. All previous conversations with her were over the phone, which had left me at a disadvantage. You see, whenever the conversation became uncomfortable for her, she would abruptly end it, and hang up. I could not stand this, since I felt helpless and frustrated because so many things were left unsaid. However, now there was no escape.

The tone I used when I spoke to her was respectful. There was no anger, there was no frustration, just a calm feeling within me. During the conversation, I asked her about certain things that had happened in the past. Having waited so long for this question, I asked her, "Why can't I remember the beatings from my father, but I remember the many beatings I got from you?" "I don't know why you can't remember," she answered, somewhat agitated. "Why would you say that you hope my children don't treat me as badly as I treated you?" "I never said that." "Well, I remember you saying it. Also, you said that Opa did not care for me because of my skin color. Oma said that Opa loved me, and that is what I remember, too." Again, she denied it. "I never said that Opa didn't care for you." Her only defense was denial. Regardless of what questions I asked her, she denied all of them.

I had to be very selective with my questions, and even so, she became very upset. Heartfelt questions, such as, *Why would you not let me live with my father? Why, according to you, was I such a bad son? Why are you so angry with me?* These were but a few of the many questions on my mind that I wanted to ask her. Of course, I had my answers, but just wanted and needed to hear what she had to say, knowing that she would have never truthfully answered those questions anyway.

Clearly, my mother's agitation was reaching a boiling point, so I decided to end the conversation. Talking to Lisa afterwards, I told her that I would give it two days before my mother would come to us and say that she had to leave. Well, I was wrong. It took only one day. The very next day, my mother informed me that she had to go back to

Germany. She said that on the way back to Germany, she would stop by her friend in Texas.

A Final Goodbye

Taking her to the airport, I walked her to the gate (before 9-11) and wished her a good flight. "Please call me when you get to Texas so I know that you are well." "Okay, I will." I knew she was lying. For some unknown reason, I felt uneasy, but could not put my finger on it. Saying goodbye, I walked away, and after a few steps, turned around to look at her again. She was sitting in a chair, looking at me. It was like in a movie, where the focus was on my mother sitting in that chair, and everything else around her vanished. I don't know how to explain what I felt at that moment, but looking at her, a deep sadness overcame me. Feeling abandonment once again, it almost crushed me. In that instant I knew, *I would never see my mother again.*

Confirmation That I Am Free

Not having spoken to my mother in seven years, I decided to call her on her birthday. "Hello Mama." "Who is this?" she answered. "This is Johnny, your son." She seemed not to know who I was. Maybe this indicated the onset of Alzheimer's, which has rendered her helpless today, as she is now in a nursing home. The content of the conversation was not important, but what was important was my reaction to her.

You see, whenever I would speak to my mother before, I would get really nervous, and I would have these butterflies in my stomach. It was a sign of nervousness, which meant I still allowed her to control me. However, during this conversation, I felt totally at peace for the first time, and knew right then that I was finally healed. I realized that the control I had allowed my mother to have over me was definitely gone.

My self-discovery journey that had started in my twenties came full circle in my thirties. The troubled relationship I'd had with my mother finally ended. As painful as this was at first, I soon realized that I was finally free! The burden of having to prove myself, the burden of trying so hard to be accepted by my mother, was lifted.

Visiting Home with Lisa and Children

Nine years after having last seen my mother, I took Lisa and our three youngest children for a visit to Germany. It was their first time, and a great opportunity to meet my best friend, Coco, my family, and to see the country I grew up in. During the stay, my children expressed an interest in seeing their grandmother. Certainly, I had no objections. Lisa called my mother. "Hi Mom, this is Lisa, John's wife. How are you? We are in town visiting with our children, and they would really like to see you." Lisa had the phone on speaker, so I could follow the conversation. My mother responded, "Oh, I would like to see the children, but I am really sick. I have the flu." She started coughing to make her point. "Sorry to hear that you are sick Mom," Lisa replied, "but maybe they can see you, just for a brief second?" Suffice it to say, though having every opportunity to say yes, she provided nothing but excuses as to why she could not see the children.

Sure, she was not feeling well, but I would think that having reduced the distance between us from 6,000 to only a couple of miles would have resulted in seeing her; yet, we still were unable to. Though my mother is still alive, my prediction of never seeing her again is still on track. She now lives in a home due to Alzheimer's. I wish her well and have much love for her. Yes, I do. It'll be explained later in the book.

Premonition

So far I have shared with you two major milestones in my life. One being that my best friend, Coco, was the catalyst to my self-discovery journey, and the other, Barry's entry into my life. At this point, I want to share another milestone with you.

In 2002, Lisa and I separated. Trying to heal, I went to Germany to stay with Coco and his family. It was a very painful time for me, because the separation had left three children behind. One day while I was standing in Coco's shop, I had a premonition. Not being pleased with the way my life was going, I knew in that instant that my life needed to, and was going to, change. I just didn't know how or when; but it was going to change. I was tired of running, tired of being confused, and tired of not knowing which direction to go.

Meeting Dr. K.

After my trip overseas, I went back to Los Angeles and reconciled with Lisa. Going back to my job as a tour guide, I met a man a short while later who would point me in the right direction. Here is a classic example of drawing into your life the things you deeply think about. I had already entertained the thought of going back to school. On a tour one day, I was approached by a tourist, a man named Dr. K, and he told me that he was the president of a university back east. "What are you doing with your life?" "I want to be a public speaker." "Have you thought about getting your master's? This will solidify your position as a speaker." "Yes, I thought about going back to school, but leaving my children in order to attend classes does not appeal to me." "Well, you know, there are very good universities which teach online. This way you will get a great education without leaving your children." "This is new to me. I had no idea." As the president of a university, I took his suggestion seriously. Long story short, I checked out some universities, Capella University in particular.

Within three months, I was enrolled at Capella University. After about six months at the university, I naïvely decided to continue and get my doctorate, even though I had just started my master's. I say naïvely, because I had no idea of the immense amount of work, time and sacrifice it would take to become a doctor. Having earned my bachelor's degree at Campbell University, I must say that the work involved at Capella was much greater. Here, I had to read all the assignments, rather than listen to a professor and take notes. In addition, the university's academic standards were very high, which meant that the curriculum was rigorous and demanding. Though I was mostly at home doing my work, I was almost invisible to my family. The workload was tremendous, and that was during the years of getting my master's. Pursuing my Ph.D., I entered an entirely different world.

Family Pictures

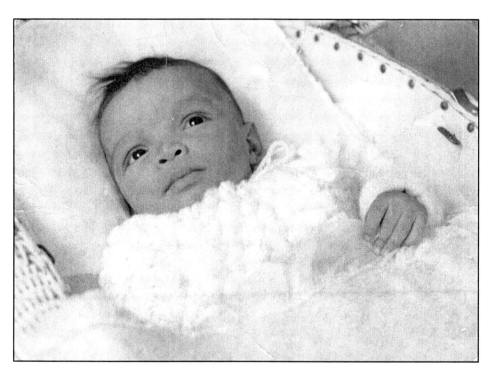

At age three months, living in a convent and cared for by nuns.
Schwäbisch Gmünd, 1961.

Flanked by my parents, at age one. Mainz, 1962.

At age six, right after the restaurant incident
just before boarding the train. Stuttgart, 1967.

My favorite picture with my Oma, at age 9.
Schwäbisch Gmünd, 1970.

On a field trip with my classmates, at age 13 (first row, fourth from right).
Most of us still enjoy a close friendship today. Germany, 1975.

Finally home again, after three long years.
At the airport, right after I landed in Frankfurt.
Germany, 1982.

*Junior year at Campbell University, doing what I enjoyed most then:
playing 'Fussball.' Buies Creek, N.C. 1983.*

*My best friend (Brother) Coco
and I enjoying a meal at a restaurant.
Heuchlingen, 2009.*

*Lisa (wife), children and I enjoying a family get-together.
Anthony, Tahi (back row), John, Tiana (middle row), and Nico (front).
Raven (next to Lisa and I) is our newly adopted daughter.
Mia, the baby, is her daughter. Los Angeles, 2012.*

Lisa and I with our first granddaughter, Mia. Los Angeles, 2012.

PART 3

Becoming a Doctor

BEGINNING MY DOCTORATE immediately after I earned my master's, I had very little vacation, because the university operated on the quarter system. That meant that I had at most two weeks (sometimes not even that long) between courses. This is a stretch of my life that was very intense, to say the least. I was very excited to start my doctorate, because I knew that I had to write a dissertation. In other words, I had to conduct my own scientific study. It was clear to me then that my study was going to be about biracial individuals. I wanted to know if the feelings I had about being biracial were shared by others. The results of the study conclusively supported my contention that biracial individuals had, and still have, difficulties being accepted, while also having to deal with racism and prejudice.

The next part of this book promises to be powerful! I will share with you some fascinating, and at times disturbing, information I discovered while conducting my own scientific study as I was earning my doctorate.

Understanding Racism

Why is racism still so prevalent in this world? Have race relations not improved? Why are people not accepted just because they are different? These are a few of the many questions I pondered. Having done major research on the subject of racism, I have come across some very interesting information. The following chapters will illustrate why racism and discrimination are difficult and unshakable issues in America. Furthermore, I present the following information to put my life struggles with being biracial into proper context. Let's take a brief trip into the past to discover the roots of racism in America. However, before we do, let's define the terms racism and discrimination.

Racism upholds the theory that intellectual or moral superiority is based on physical appearance. It promotes the negative evaluation and rejection of people mainly because of their skin color.

Discrimination is defined as activities that disqualify members of one group from opportunities open to others as a result of deep prejudice held by individuals (or groups). It is a daily occurrence for countless people of color, which the majority of White people will never experience.

Modern slavery is said to have begun between the fifteen and sixteenth centuries. In America, White superiority became the norm. It justified slavery, the extermination of Indians, and the taking of Mexican land. People of color were seen as second-class citizens. The fact that my great-grandparents weren't allowed to marry because he was White and she was part Choctaw Indian, is an example of being treated as second-class citizens.

George Washington

America was founded on the principle that all men are created equal. But I ask you: how is that possible when George Washington, the founding father, was a slave owner? Clearly, one can see the hypocrisy in this historical fact. Are all men truly created equal? I think not! Rather, it means: all *White* men are created equal. As history has proven, the implications that George Washington was a slave owner were profound and far-reaching then, and still are today.

Dr. Benjamin Rush

Adding to the plight, the mental health field has shown its unfavorable treatment of people of color. Incredibly, psychiatry has done much damage regarding racism, and here again we have a prominent figure playing a major role.

Dr. Benjamin Rush is considered the 'father' of American psychiatry. He declared that skin color of Blacks was caused by a rare disease called Negritude. The sign of a cure, according to Rush, was only when the skin turned white. Coming across this information was stunning, to say the least. Here is another celebrated figure doing incredible damage to the understanding of people of color, especially black people. Rush might have not dared to make this statement had he realized that white skin color was, and actually is, the minority on this planet. Yes, people of color dominate. We are the majority, NOT the minority. Then again, maybe he knew exactly what he was doing. Unfortunately, it gets worse.

The most amazing claim Rush made was that skin color affected the IQ. Simply put, it meant that people of color were inferior to white people. This lie encouraged and kept segregation alive and well, while also discouraging people to intermarry, thus further encouraging racial segregation. Why would such a prominent doctor make such devastating statements? Why would such a person lie? Was he really unaware, simply that ignorant, or were his statements a deliberate plan to keep people of color in control? Believe me, I have pondered these questions extensively. Yes, I have arrived at answers, but that is an entirely different topic, and would go beyond the purpose of this book.

Civil Rights

To further support my position that racism and discrimination are difficult and unshakable issues in America, consider the following facts: it was not until 1954 that segregation in public schools was deemed unconstitutional with the Supreme Court ruling in Brown v. Board of Education. It was not until 1964, with the Civil Rights Act, that discrimination of all kinds based on color, race, religion, or national origin became illegal. It was not until 1965 that people of color were allowed to vote (Voting Rights Act of 1965). Finally, it was not until 1967 that people of different races were able to marry. The Supreme Court in Loving v. Virginia overruled the law against inter-racial marriage because it deemed these laws unconstitutional under the Fourteenth Amendment.

One can hardly argue the impact that George Washington, the founding father of the United States, had on America. One can hardly dispute that Dr. Benjamin Rush's declarations are not only false, but outright slanderous. Lastly, one can hardly disagree that because the Civil Rights laws were only put into effect in recent history, racism and discrimination are still major forces in America.

It is not my intention, nor desire, to fill this book with a plethora of historical information about the racist tendencies of America; however, this information is crucial to understanding the situation I dealt with while growing up, since both Germany and America were (white) mono-racial societies. Logically, if I was confronted with this way of life, it is safe to assume that other people of color, were as well. As you continue to read on, it will become clear why this world is still overrun with racial tension.

Historical Development of the Biracial Population

It is a fact that historically, biracial individuals were not accepted by society. It is also my personal experience. To discourage people from race-mixing (African slaves or Native Americans and English settlers), anti-miscegenation laws were passed in the Colonies in the late fifteenth century. This law made interracial marriages illegal (i.e., my great-grandparents) for many generations (until Loving v. Virginia, 1967). Many people believed that not only were interracial marriages unnatural and against the will of God, but the children from interracial unions were considered to be physically and mentally deficient. Furthermore, people believed these children would biologically lower the superior European race.

The last two statements are powerful. Is this the reason I was treated with disrespect when the waiter refused to serve me potato soup, even though I was just a little boy? Certainly, I was no physical threat to him. Was it his contempt for me because he felt that I was 'contaminating' his race? You decide.

As if life wasn't already backbreaking enough, another law put into effect during slavery was the hypo-descent rule. Also known as the 'one-drop' rule, it declared that racially-mixed children were relegated to the racial group of the lower-status parent, regardless of physical appearance. That explains why I was called Schwarzer, even though my mother was White.

The population of biracial individuals dramatically increased after the 1967 Supreme Court ruling, Loving v. Virginia. This decision had far-reaching implications. Read these next lines carefully. At one point in history, 41 out of 50 states in America had laws against interracial marriage in place. Even more incredible is that Alabama did not officially ban the law against interracial marriage from its state constitution until 2000. More incredibly, even then, 40 percent of the Alabama people who voted were against eliminating the ban of interracial marriage from the state constitution.

Now, this is unreal. If you doubt my previous claim that racism is an unshakable issue in America, partly because Civil Rights laws weren't put into effect until recent history, is 2000 recent enough? Better yet, allow me to give you another example of how deeply ingrained racism is in America, even today.

Fact is, President Obama is **not** the first black president of the United States of America. He is biracial (father black, mother white); Obama is the first person of color who is President of the United States; yet he's referred to as a Black president. What about the other half, the white half of his heritage? Why is it ignored? It is my opinion that most people in the Black and White community ignore Obama's White heritage, but for two different reasons. The Black community seems to delight in the fact that a man with part Black heritage is the President of the United States of America, boosting the Black community's self-esteem and pride. Understandable. The White community seems to ignore Obama's White heritage as if to say, regardless of your White heritage, and despite being the President of the United States of America, you are still Black! This is, in my opinion, a clear message if there ever was one. So deeply ingrained is racism in this society that society cannot, *will* not, rightfully and correctly acknowledge a person's true racial background.

Society Determines Race

It has been my personal experience that being biracial in itself is not a problem. Studies have shown this to be the case. Rather, it is people's reaction to it. Regardless of how I view myself, it is society that determines how I am classified. This in turn left me no choice but to refer to myself as Black, and ignore my white heritage. Psychologically, I paid dearly for having to make that choice. Though it seems making a choice as to one's heritage is still necessary today, it has no affect on me anymore. I'll get to that a little later.

Not once while growing up, even in the presence of my mother, was I ever referred to as White. I was always Black. Well, there is one exception, and a story worth sharing with you.

Mr. DMV

Campbell, the first university I attended, is located within the small community Buies Creek, in North Carolina. Many students got involved with the community, and it was no different for us players of the soccer team. Not only did many of us volunteer for Special Olympics twice a year, but several players on my team volunteered to coach the children's community soccer teams. It was a great experience, as over the years we saw girls and boys become young women and young men.

I bonded well with the kids and parents alike. The father of one of my players worked for the Department of Motor Vehicles (DMV). He was a kind, southern, white man, and treated me with great respect. He was very fond of me. It was time to renew my driver's license, and he was the one to help me. After going through the normal procedure, it came to the part where I had to state my race. Being used to this, I automatically told him to put down Black. I have thought about what happened next countless times, to figure out why he reacted the way he did, but am still indecisive. You form your own opinion.

As if he were insulted by my claim of being black, he responded in an almost angry way, "You are not Black!" "Well, that is what I have always been classified as," I responded. "John, you are not black. I am not putting this on your driver's license. Tell me, what race are your parents?" "My father is black and my mother is white." "Your mother is white?" he excitedly asked me. "Yes, she is." "Then that is what you are. You are White. That is what I am putting on your driver's license."

It took my breath away. Here was a southern white man who refused to see me as anything but White. I had read and knew about the white southern man's reputation regarding Black people. Analyzing this incident many times over, I arrived at two possibilities. Either this man was so fond of me, that the thought of liking a black man was not acceptable to him, so he had to justify his feelings in some way. When I told him my mother was white, he took that statement and ran with it. He may still be running. Then again, having a European upbringing, I may not have acted like an American, which may be the reason he proclaimed that I was not Black. Either way I look at it, I find it amazing. The great thing is, I still have that North Carolina driver's license. I am looking at it right now, and under the box Race/Sex, it reads WM...White Male!

Having to Choose

I am positive that feeling the pressure of having to choose one heritage over another resulted in my suffering from low self-esteem. Equally so, I suffered from a severe case of identity crisis, and it did not help that there wasn't a role model in my life. As an adolescent growing up in Germany, I had to periodically answer the question by German authorities what race I identified with. I answered that I considered myself Black, mirroring society's acceptance of me. This enraged my mother, who insisted to them that I was not Black.

I did not understand the impact of the situation then, and I can only imagine how my mother must have felt. Claiming that I was Black simply negated the other half of my heritage; it negated my mother. Imagine the psychological implications of turning your back on your mother or father because you have to choose one race over the other.

If information received about oneself is that of acceptance, respect and approval, multiracial people will most likely acquire a healthy, positive self-esteem. On the other hand, they are likely to develop a low or unhealthy self-esteem if important people in their lives, like family members or close friends, reject or belittle them. This is what my mother had done all my life. Hearing only negative things about my father and black people, it continued with belittling me at every opportunity. Is there a wonder my self-esteem was low?

Differently put, how biracial individuals come to understand themselves is powerfully influenced by other people's opinion of them. How well people respond to biracial individuals plays a big part in how they respond to themselves. "Oh, people like me. Then I must be okay. So I can like myself," or, "Oh, people don't like me. Something must be wrong with me." Well, from the comments I received from my mother, something was seriously wrong with me.

Another dilemma for biracial individuals is the fact that it is not uncommon for them to be rejected as full members of the minority community. My personal experience, supported by the results of my doctoral study, confirmed just that. Not only do many biracial people find themselves being minorities within larger society, many find themselves to be a minority within the minority community. Many are simply not accepted as full members.

Some of the participants in my research addressed exactly this point. One participant, who is Black and White, stated that she was told many times by Black family members that she was not Black enough. A different participant, who is of Korean and El Salvadorian descent, shared with me that the Korean community felt that he was not Korean enough to be accepted as a full member. Even more tragic for him, his father rejected and abandoned him. I was, and still am, often considered too light to be Black. In fact, when people guess what ethnicity I am, Black is usually never part of the equation, which begs the 'famous' question: what are you?

What Am I?

The question, "What are you?" is one of the most-often questions I am asked. It does three things: first, it denotes that I (e.g., biracial individual) must define myself in some way. The emphasis is on *must*. Second, it compounds the issue that the given answer never seems good enough; thus, internalizing the message that I am not good enough, and therefore do not belong. Third, being of mixed heritage provides evidence of racial impurity.

What makes this situation more complicated for multiracial people is that society does not offer unambiguous and reliable guidelines for racial identification. Consider the use of blood as criterion for assigning racial identity: Native American individuals must prove a blood quantum to be regarded as Native American. Yet, it takes only one drop of Black blood to be regarded as Black. Think about that.

As the above information shows, the psychological cost of racism on minorities is tremendous. Constantly bombarded on all sides that Whites and their way of life are superior, and all other lifestyles are inferior, many minorities see themselves as unworthy or inadequate.

This is how I felt. The mass media does its part to perpetuate and rein-force the inferior status of minorities through television, newspapers, magazines, movies, radio, and books.

As a result, stereotypical beliefs about minorities abound, char-acterizing Blacks as superstitious, ignorant, dangerous or criminals. Hispanics are portrayed as dirty, sneaky, and criminal, and Asians as sneaky, sly, cunning, or passive. Native American Indians do not fare better, being depicted as primitive savages. Can one really wonder then that people of color are not negatively affected by such non-sense? There seems no escape.

Having earned my doctorate undoubtedly gives me a sense of accomplishment. Notwithstanding, I also know that this is just the beginning of my next journey; a journey of not only helping people of color to improve the quality of their lives by accepting themselves, re-gardless of what society dictates, but also helping people who suffer from low self-esteem, lack of self-love or lack of social acceptance, to reach their full potential.

PART 4

Accepting Myself

IT'S BEEN A long journey, but I have come to accept myself. I often have conversations with people who claim to be happy with themselves. They say they are happy with who they are, and where they are in life; yet, they complain about certain people in their lives, or certain situations that happened in the past. How can it be that one accepts oneself totally, but does not accept everything in the past? I put forth the argument then that if one truly loves who she or he is, then everything in the past, people and situations, should also be accepted by that person.

I love who I am and who I have become. I understand that my past, people and situations, have allowed me to become who I am today. I would not change a thing. There were a great many people in my life who had a positive influence on me, just as there were some who had a negative influence on me. There were people in my life who told me that I would never amount to anything (I wish I could have invited them to my graduation ceremony to see me get my Ph.D.). Nevertheless, it is those people who had a negative influence that helped me appreciate the wonderful things in life even more.

A great example would be my mother. Treating me the way she did showed me how *not* to treat people, especially my wife and children. I like to believe that I am a better husband and father, in spite of the way she treated me. I am a better parent because of her. All the things that I lacked from her such as love, comfort, protection, nurturing, etc., I provide for my children, and the love and support I did not get from her, I give to my wife Lisa. So instead of carrying hatred around, which in the end only hurts the person who's doing the hating, I let go. I recognize that in order for me to appreciate what it means to be without, I had to experience it firsthand.

Understand, I love my mother. I do not hate her. I realize that my mother has been one of my greatest teachers. If I were to carry the hatred or grudge within my heart, I would not be able to love my wife and children, and treat them the way they deserve to be treated. In the end, all of us will have to come to terms with the things we did and said. I believe there is no escaping from that. Being bitter is like a disease, and will eat you up, unless you let go of it.

Though I have forgiven my mother, I have not forgotten the things she did, and the hurtful words she spoke. I choose not to forget, simply because it keeps me on guard. It serves as a reminder that I will not allow anybody to treat me the way I was treated before. And it serves as a reminder to treat people with love and respect. It is everybody's right to be treated with love and respect. After all, this is what we all want in one form or another, is it not?

I Am Who I Am

As far as how I was treated in Germany, I have come to terms with that also. It doesn't matter anymore whether Germans accept me, or for that matter, any society. I am who I am. I am neither Black nor White. I am me! Having learned that countless people are multiracial, whether they know it or not, has lessened my desire to be categorized. Truth be told, I am not even biracial. If you remember reading about my great-grandparents at the beginning of the book, it is written that my great-grandfather was of Irish and Scottish descent, and my great-grandmother of (unknown) White and Choctaw Indian descent. That makes me a person of multiracial descent.

You may ask then how I came to make peace with my past. Hard and honest work is my answer. I confronted the emotions and people associated with them that caused me so much grief over many years. In order for me to heal, I had to admit that something was not right. I had to allow myself to feel my real emotions. The key was to confront the people who hurt me without expectations; meaning, I was not expecting them to apologize or understand. If they did, great. If they did not, so be it. Just being able to get these draining and negative emotions out of my system was a wonderful feeling; a way of healing. This meant that I went through periods where I was sad, angry, hurt, and depressed. I needed to go through all these feelings, all these emotions, if I was ever going to heal from this pain. I realized that if I were to hold them in, ignore them, or pretend everything was okay, I was fooling myself. Yes, I fooled many people, but in the end, I could not fool myself.

What made it easier for me to realize that my relationship with my mother was not healthy was the fact that every time, yes *every* time, we had arguments, I was the one who had to make up. There was only one time when she approached me and apologized, only one. When I was eleven years old, she hit me in my left eye with a shoe. The next day, I felt what seemed like a rain drop streaking across my left eyeball. It was not until some friends told me that there was blood in my eye that I realized it was not a raindrop. When I showed the blood-streaked eyeball to my mother, she seemed to feel sorry, and actually apologized. That was the only time she ever did!

There were times when I did not want to make up, because she was clearly at fault; but it was my family, usually one of my aunts, who insisted I should make up. They would say things like, "Johnny, this is your mother. You only have one." "I know that, but she is wrong and I am tired of always having to be the one to make up," I would respond. "Johnny, she may not have been right in the way she handled herself, but you are her only son. Please, just talk to her."

Talk about making someone feel guilty! I am her *only son,* as if I did not know this. This is society's way (in this case, probably more Catholic guilt) of making people believe they are obligated to family members. I have no problem with honoring obligations of family ties. However, if the family ties are detrimental to oneself, I believe in not honoring those ties. I feel the same way about honoring parents. The Bible says to honor your parents. I say yes, if they honor you, the child, also. If they do not honor you, I see no obligation to honor the parents.

This does not mean you should talk badly about your parents, or for that matter, anyone else. It means to stay out of harm's way in whatever form, fashion or shape that you believe to be healthy. Previously, I stated that my mother used to say, "I am your mother and I am always right." What I have not disclosed is that my father believed something similar. Though I am convinced that he shared my mother's opinion, he added a different angle to it. After a disagreement one day, he said, "I am your father. *You* come to *me*, not the other way around." Here again, we have this belief that children are to always honor their parents. And as I stated before, I agree. However, I do not agree when it is not mutual, and that is exactly what I told my father.

Some of you readers may disagree with me. That is fine. You have your own way of dealing with your friends and family, and you have your own method of healing. This is my method, and it is a method that has worked, and still works, for me. You see, I love family, friends, people and myself. What I realized though is that in order for me to really love others, I must love myself first. If I do not, then loving others cannot be the real deal. The love you have for others must come from you. Not because you feel obligated, are convinced by others you have to, or because of guilt.

You Are in Charge

It has been my experience that some people do not like being special; that is, they do not accept that they are special, for it would require them to stand up and take responsibility for their life. To avoid taking responsibility, they simply become followers. Being a follower allows them the luxury to blame others for the conditions in their life.

It allows them to blame others (e.g., friends, spouse, parents, God) for all the things they do not like. What they fail to realize, however, is that they are giving their power away. It is a power that is within every person. It has always been, and it will always be.

So it is with decisions. By not making a decision you, whether you believe it or not, make a decision, nonetheless. You allow yourself to be led, and though you may blame someone later for being led down the wrong path, it is *you* who decided not to make a decision. It is *you* who made the decision. It is *you* who made the decision not to make a decision. So either way you look at it, it is you, and only you, who decides the faith of your journey.

Okay to Be Bifferent

It has taken me many years to realize that being different is a good thing. I will admit that it is not easy. I have found that some people do all they can to hold others back. They criticize people's uniqueness because of their fear of embracing their own uniqueness. No two people are alike. We are all different. Therefore, who is to decide who is acceptable, or for that matter, undesirable? What's more, who decides that being different is a bad thing?

I now am aware that being different makes us special. I did not say better, I said special. EVERYONE is special. There is nothing wrong with acknowledging this. I do not want to be like others, nor should you want to be like others. It would defeat our purpose of being here on this planet. Just like we are different from everyone else, so are our likes, desires, opinions, values, and dreams unlike any other person's. What we have come here for is different from what others are here for. In other words, what we have come here to accomplish in this lifetime, no other will accomplish. That, my friends, is special!

Believe in Yourself

Believe in yourself. You need to understand that no matter what others say, it is your opinion, the opinion you have of yourself, that counts more than anybody's. No matter what religion, what sexual orientation, whether you are short or tall, whether society thinks you are beautiful or not. However, the opinion you have of yourself must be loving, kind, and accepting. If it is not, all else will be counterproductive. You get my point?

Please Yourself First

You cannot please everyone. You are not supposed to please everyone. That, by nature, is impossible to do. Pleasing *yourself* should be the objective. Some of you may not agree, saying that is selfish. Yes, it is. Society has taught people that looking out for oneself is wrong and selfish. I disagree. However, we are not talking about *only* thinking and pleasing yourself. Pleasing others is a wonderful thing to do, and should be the aim of everyone, of course. But before you can please anyone, you must know how to please yourself. How else will you understand what it means to please? It's the same with love. How are you truly able to love someone else, if you don't know how to love yourself? Let that soak in for a moment.

There was a time when I was trying to please everyone, especially my mother. You know what? It was exhausting. Eventually, I realized that there was no pleasing my mother, and I realized that no matter what I did, I was unable to please society. What made me grasp that I was on the wrong path were two things: some people were complaining that I did not do enough for them regardless of what I did. That was disappointing. Two, I started getting sick from all this people-pleasing; sick physically and mentally. I got to the point where I said, *enough is enough!*

So I started to take care of myself more, and stopped pleasing everyone. As a result, I became healthier. It was like a big weight was lifted off my shoulders. Furthermore, believe it or not, people started to show more respect towards me. They saw how I took care of myself and respected myself, hence, they respected me. Yes, there were some who complained, and even ended the friendship. Though hard at first, eventually I understood that **they were not my friends to begin with.**

I shared this little story with you to help you understand that no matter what circumstances in your life have led others to not accept you, it does not mean that you have to do the same. Accept yourself! Jealousy and envy are part of this world. We cannot control what and how others think of us. Nonetheless, we can control how we react. Either you let this nonsense influence you negatively, or you understand and shrug off their negativity. You do not have to try to win them over. You can let them go, release them from your life. No matter who they may be. Yes, even if they are family.

You are a precious being who deserves all the best that life has to offer. Whether you choose to accept or not to accept all the best that life has to offer is your choice. You don't have to, nor should you let other people choose for you, because one of the greatest powers you have is the power of choice. Either you choose, or you don't. And no my friends, such a journey is not easy, but remember, when all else fails, the only person who stays with you throughout your entire life, is you. So accept, love and treat yourself with respect. If you can do this for you, you can do it for others, too. Pleasing others then comes from a place of love, and not a place of insecurity. It comes from strength, not weakness. It comes from you, not others.

You Have a Purpose

There is a reason why you are here. There is a purpose why you are here. There is a reason and a purpose why you are you. Allow me to share the following with you. When I look back at my life, I understand now how everything I went through prepared me for this moment. You see, at one time, I thought I would become a professional soccer player. I did not. Then I found my way into the entertainment industry. With the connections I had, I surely was going to succeed. I did not. Though I wanted to be a professional soccer player, and wanted to succeed in the entertainment industry, I did not. They key word here is: wanted. It was not meant to be.

What I did finally realize is that we may not always get what we want, but we will always get what we need. The reason for that is, because whether we know it or not, we are following our purpose for being here. We may not like it, at least at first, but it is the way it is. C'est la vie, again.

One thing that has been consistent throughout my life is that I was involved with teaching or serving people, one way or another. You see, my passion is people. So here I am before you, today doing what I love to do most: being of service to you. So you, too, have a purpose for being here. To find out your purpose might require a little soul-searching. The help of trusted others will ease your search, but only you can truly find out what your reason and purpose is. Only you will know what your true purpose on this planet is. **Only you!**

To be continued...

CPSIA information can be obtained at www.ICGtesting.com
Printed in the USA
BVOW010251040213

312313BV00007B/63/P

9 781478 716693